FAITH THROUGH FIRE: RWANDA AND ME

THE MEMOIR OF
GARY BENNETT
BY RANDALL E. BENNETT

Copyright © 2012 Randall E. Bennett
All rights reserved.
ISBN: 1478342595
ISBN 13: 9781478342595
Library of Congress Control Number: 2012914053
CreateSpace, North Charleston, SC

Gary and Randy wish to acknowledge the encouragement of their wives in completing this project. We could not have completed this project without the assistance, love, and support of our awesome wives, Barb and Amy!

This book is dedicated to the memory of Lillian and of course, Melanie.

TABLE OF CONTENTS

1. Birdsong 1
2. Only Nine Months 5
3. In God's Hands Now 13
4. Banana Bread 21
5. Bringing in the Tent 27
6. The Beard 31
7. Refuge 35
8. The Call 41
9. Preparations 45
10. Into the Water 51
11. On the Move 59
12. The Jesus Film 67
13. Refusing to Go 77
14. Blind Date 85
15. No Colleague Left Behind 93
16. The List 103
17. A Dangerous Mission 111
18. Embers 121
19. Night 131
20. The Beginning 135
21. My Hiding Place 143
22. Tensions Rising 151
23. The Legionnaires 157
24. Static 167
25. Going Back 169
26. Searching 173
27. Shredded Pieces 175
28. Survival 179
29. Curtains 183
30. Reunion 189

31	Found	193
32	Seeing is Believing	197
33	A Walk of Faith	199
34	The Future	205
35	A Business Venture	209
36	Hope Comes In Tiny Bundles	213
37	An Unexpected Turn	215
38	A Halo	219
39	Pulling Away	221
40	Not Afraid	225
41	With and Without	229
42	No Regrets	233
43	Friends	237
44	Prayer and Singing	243
45	Afterword	247

BIRDSONG

APRIL 6, 1994
KIGALI, RWANDA

A place has never been so silent; a place has never been so loud.

Normally, in the early morning we would have been hearing signs of life as people prepared themselves for the day. Voices greeting each other. Children playing. Dogs barking. Automobiles moving down the street. The clang of pans on stoves as morning meals are prepared. And the birds. By that hour the birds are always full swing into their usual throaty racket. Mouse tails, robin chats and all manner of tropical birds share our neighborhood. But this morning, something was different. There was no music. No human voice. Even the tropical birds had been stilled. And the noises I was hearing now did not make sense. No sense at all.

Gunfire, then a grenade. Gunfire, grenade.

When I first realized that the gunfire we had been hearing on and off for the last hour was in close proximity to us—on our very street even—I looked over at Melanie. She paused to look back at me through the frames of her glasses. She was concerned, but there was little sign of fear in her eyes; no panic. She only nodded once at me and made to leave the room.

"You stay here in the hallway," I told her, following her out. My thoughts raced through the possible scenarios of what might be happening outside our door. How Melanie could be acting so calm was beyond me. From all outward appearances, she acted as if nothing extraordinary were going on at all. Was she really not afraid?

I took a deep breath, letting my own panic settle within me as I drew from the example of her faith. God would protect us, I was sure of it. All of my life I have had the deeply ingrained sense that God protects His own. It was not that I was under the illusion that nothing bad ever happens to His followers, but I reminded myself that nothing happens to them without His permission. I paused to consider what this actually meant. That was when I noticed the sound Melanie's feet made as she made her way down the hallway toward the kitchen. She had put on her shoes.

Shots fired directly across the street from us spurred me into action. I jammed my own feet into a pair of shoes and slipped out the front door. Many of the homes in the Rwandan capital of Kigali are surrounded by an eight-foot high brick wall and topped with broken glass, ours included. I have never before been so grateful for its existence. In the middle of the rainy season, the ground was still spongy as the heavy morning humidity hung in the air and condensed on everything it touched. I walked closely alongside the wall that surrounds our home. I stepped up onto an overturned crate for leverage and peeked over the wall.

Two government soldiers bearing AK 47s stood outside the small house across the street. As I waited, I heard more shots inside the house. After a few moments, two more men appeared wearing the patterned garb distinct to the Interahamwe, the local citizen militia. One of them was wearing an army jacket. I barely had time to ask myself why this would be, when one of the Interahamwe men pulled a grenade out from a pouch on his waist, pulled the pin, and tossed it into the house. The four of them jogged to the street as the inside of the house flashed and blew dark debris out through the windows. The men made their way down the street to the next house and went inside.

Stepping down, I pressed my back against the wall, uncertain of what to do. Uncertain of what I *could* do. My neighbors were dead, I was sure of it. I knew them. They were a pleasant family, always friendly to Melanie and me. With their height and distinct, delicate facial bone structure, we had known they were Tutsi, sure. It is not difficult to tell most Tutsis apart from their shorter, broader featured Hutu neighbors. Their ethnic background had never made the slightest difference to us. To most of them, their ethnic background had never made any difference to each other. But things had been changing. Now, it seemed everything had changed.

From the moment I woke up that morning, I knew something was wrong. Turning my head, I glanced at the clock by the bed. A quarter after five. My wife Melanie was beside me, sound asleep finally after the uncertain night. The evening before, we had heard two loud explosions from the direction of the airport. We were used to gunfire, noises in the distance. This was different. A call from the US Embassy warned us of a rumor that the president's plane had been shot down.

"Stay alert," the voice had told us over the phone. "Prepare for possible evacuation."

We gathered a few things together. I stashed the computer up in the attic. We threw a change of clothes, deodorant, passports and money into a bag.

Evacuation: the act of leaving a place empty.

What would we take? Our lives were here. Rwanda had been my home on and off for the previous nineteen years. I was not ready to leave this place empty. I was not ready to leave at all.

I strained to listen in the dark. Only the sound of my own blood as it coursed through my veins throbbed in my ears. *What happened to the radio?* I had wondered. We had left it on all night, waiting for news. The government station, Radio Rwanda, had been playing classical music throughout the early morning hours, already an indication that something was not right. But now everything was still. The horizon was just beginning to brighten as dawn approached.

That's when it came. A voice was speaking in a low, clear and somber tone. It was a male voice on the radio, speaking in Kinyarwanda.

"*Umukuru w'igihugu yapfuye barashe indege yari arimo.*" *Our beloved president died when his plane was shot down last night.*

The capital city of Kigali compressed like the first moments of a nuclear explosion. There was an inhalation of breath, a pause, a detonation.

When the city erupted in explosions and gunfire, I was too stunned to move. Melanie, awake now beside me, reached for my hand. Lying frozen in our bed, waves of adrenalin washed over and through us as hundreds — *thousands* — of guns were fired into the air across the city. It lasted for several minutes. And then it was over. All was still. But the beast that would feed on flesh and soul had only just been unleashed. It was only gathering more breath.

Little did I know then what the extent of the damage would be.

Little did I know then what I would be forced to confront in my own life.

We would not again hear the serene voices of the birds of Rwanda for four months.

ONLY NINE MONTHS

OCTOBER 1975
WINDOM, MN / GISENYI, RWANDA

When I first left for Africa in October of 1975, I had no intention of ever becoming a missionary. I was raised on the fresh, industrious air of a Minnesota farm. I think this helped create a hearty personality in me. I was young and energetic and I was ready for an adventure.

While I'll admit it now — that it was primarily for the thrill of it — I told my folks a slightly edited version of the truth. I spoke to my father first.

"It's what God wants me to do," I told him after explaining that I was going to Rwanda to help a missionary family with a building project. The missionary family was friends of ours through the local church. I went to college with their son, Judd. Judd was like me in some ways: 5'10", medium build, and with a heart for God. Unlike me, he had grown up in Africa and had thousands of foreign adventures under his belt. Walking around campus together or holed up in the dormitory late at night, I was awestruck by his stories. They compelled me.

Dad and I were out in the garage changing an alternator on a large Freightliner. It was my father's semi, one of several he drove for his trucking business—the same business he had hoped I would take over from him some day.

"How long?" he asked straining only slightly against a wrench positioned on one of the bolts. As usual, he was dressed in a white T-shirt, a pair of jeans and a dirty cap over his bald spot that read "Taylor and Martin Auctioneers." The T-shirt was freshly grease-stained, a badge of pride for my father that proved he had been working. At age 53, he was still as strong as an ox and thrived on that hard work. It defined him. Aside from his standard Sunday afternoon nap after church each week, I never saw him rest.

"Only nine months," I told him. "It's just a short-term mission project. I'll be back."

"Hm," he grunted in response.

And that's the last we spoke of it until the day I left and he broke down sobbing. The entire breakfast table was sniffling, actually: my four brothers, my sister and my mother.

My dear mother. I couldn't help but steal a peek at her while we said grace. Dad was praying and she had her eyes squeezed tight, very obviously trying not to break down. I watched helplessly as she pressed her quivering lips into a line. My brother Randy looked across the table at me as if to say, "You see what you started?"

Mortified, I looked back at him and shrugged, fighting down my own tears. What could I say? We were supposed to be praying, after all.

Afterwards, they all drove me to the airport in Minneapolis. Even in the car, Dad didn't actually say anything about it. He didn't try to argue with me or convince me to stay. He had raised all six of us to think ahead, use our minds and to love God. He was letting me, his oldest, go, even though it was very clear that I had broken his heart with the decision. Even so, he had the attitude that he was in no position to question what surely seemed to be the will of God. My mother, a short but solid woman from good German stock and more talkative than my father, hugged me firmly and promised me through damp eyes that she would write regularly—a promise she kept faithfully until my return.

My friend, Judd Kile, was going to come over later so I boarded the plane by myself. I was going to meet up with an elderly missionary couple I knew in Chicago O'Hare and then head over the waters with them. First to Amsterdam, then on to Nairobi, and finally on to Kigali, the capital city of Rwanda.

Rwanda. What did I know about this underdeveloped country the size of Vermont and set in the heart of Africa? Judd had told me a little. The weather was ideal with temperatures in the 80s every day of the year. There were two rainy seasons and two dry seasons. I knew there were lions and hippos in the game parks. Diane Fossi, the eccentric Gorilla Lady I had read about in National Geographic had a house there and was occasionally spotted around the small town to which I was going. The locals were said to be friendly. I spoke neither French, nor Swahili nor the local language, Kinyarwanda, so I would have to rely largely on translators and hand gestures to get around. Food would be locally grown with kidney beans, yams and fresh fruit at the top of the menu. And, of course, there would be no electricity or running water where I was headed. In short, I knew I would be challenged at every turn.

It was exactly the adventure I was looking for.

When we touched down in Kigali on the one narrow runway at the "International" Airport, I looked out the window of the plane at the tropical trees, flowers and mud huts surrounding the property.

As I disembarked, I paused at the top of stairs. I smelled the air. *Welcome to the Third World*, I said to myself as I stepped off the plane onto dry, cracked earth.

I walked across the tarmac, through the small rectangular terminal next to the hangar, and straight into the back of a 3-ton Toyota Dyna truck owned by E.J., Judd's father.

E.J. Kile and I spent the first two days in Kigali to stock up on supplies. The first order of business, he explained, was to fill up the four 55-gallon drums in the back of the truck with gasoline for the mission's vehicles in Gisenyi. As I leaned over to check the air in the truck's tires, someone grabbed the billfold from my back pocket and tried to take off running. Fortunately, the chain from the billfold to my belt was strong. Unfortunately, the force of the guy grabbing and running caused me to fall backward and I ended up on my butt. I learned my first valuable lesson and was more cautious after that.

After two days of stocking up on food and building supplies, we were ready to leave for Gisenyi. We loaded up the truck just as the sun peeked over the horizon. As it was a single cab truck, there wasn't room for me up front so I was in the back with the boy chauffeur, or *kingingi*, whose job was to keep people from climbing on the slow moving truck to steal things as we maneuvered our way through the one thousand hills that make up Rwanda. After about five miles of tar road we turned off on a red clay dirt road. From there, I attempted to maintain my seating for the next ten hours over bumpy, dusty roads until we reached our destination of the small town of Gisenyi.

For the next nine months Judd's parents, Tudy and E.J., were my lifeline. Tudy, a petite woman with endless energy and a short, wavy crop of graying brown hair, is a nurse by training. Upon my arrival, she wasted no time in adopting me lovingly and efficiently into her brood.

"Let's get some food in you," she told me. "Be sure and wash your hands first. After that trip, there is no telling what you've touched."

Dutifully, I walked over to the sink and splashed my dusty face as well.

"If you want to stay well here, this is your most important lesson," she lectured from behind, attempting to look stern but with a little smile playing at the corner of her lips. "Stay clean. Don't drink the water unless it's been boiled and put through the filter, and don't wash with it. We have to collect what we have off the roof and from nearby springs, so don't waste it when you've got it. Respect the water. In the morning, E.J. can take you to bathe in the lake." She paused to look sternly between her husband and me. "It's all about the water."

When I was done scrubbing off what I could from the dirty trip, she brought out a feast with meat, rice, kidney beans, vegetables and a seemingly endless supply of fruit. I was starving after the trip, and grateful for every bite.

After supper, E.J. led me to the small, round stone building where I would be staying and what would become my weekend base camp when Judd and I were not working out at the site. As Gisenyi is at the base of several volcanoes, the hut was made out of volcanic rock with thick, round walls and topped with a tile roof.

Alone in my bed on the night of my arrival, I remember fighting back waves of homesickness. Staring up at the woven grass ceiling, I said a brief prayer, something along the lines of, "Well, Lord, here I am. What in the world have I gotten myself into?"

The next day the Kiles took me out to the work site across the lake. The plan was that we would stay there together for a few days so that I could get oriented, and then we would come back to the house in Gisenyi for the weekend.

Lake Kivu is a massive body of water nearly sixty miles long on Rwanda's western edge and shares borders with Congo. The terrain around

Gisenyi is made of steep hills densely covered in vegetation and the roads are difficult to travel by vehicle. To get to our work site in Cyimbili, only ten miles away as the crow flies required driving twent-five miles on dirt roads crossing twenty-six log bridges and, according to the Kiles, we were sure to fall through at least one of them.

Thus, we traveled by boat.

E.J. and Tudy took me and the other missionary couple out on my first trip over the water. We were riding on a seven-ton barge, homemade from the pole used as a rudder to the car engine that propelled it forward. E.J. stood about 5'10", weighed in at about 180 pounds and had graying hair that he would comb over his bald spot. Since he wasn't teaching at the Bible school that day, he was dressed in his work clothes — jeans and a casual button up.

"Place was left to us by a Russian gal," he told us above the drone of the engine, referring to the ninety acre coffee plantation where we would set to work renovating the house that they would move to once we were finished. "She's gone back now, of course. The plantation is still operational. You can help with that," he said to me.

I nodded and looked around at the steep hills covered with both tropical trees and cultivated land. Little round houses with thatched roofs or the newer rectangular mud block houses with shiny tin roofs peeked out from the trees in clusters. Occasionally a flash of feathers would catch my eye. I thought about the Gorilla Lady and wondered if she was out there somewhere.

"Tudy's got us taken care of for meals, but we'll have to collect our own water," E.J. called over the noisy engine. He nodded toward a couple of jerry cans sitting next to the cold boxes Tudy had sent with us. The boxes were filled with food. Next to that were an assortment of tools and various pieces of equipment. Tudy, dressed in a simple dress and sensible shoes, looked over at me and smiled.

I watched E.J., now absorbed in maneuvering the barge. My family had been friends with the Kiles for years, catching up with them as they returned on furloughs, or "home assignments." I had heard the stories of their work in Rwanda for so long that I almost had begun taking them for granted. Now that I was here, though, I was struck with the realness of it all. The struggle for basic everyday survival nearly overwhelmed me. Seeing these people in their element now—actively working toward improving the lives of their fellow humans—a true sense of awe and respect began growing inside of me.

We docked on a jetty E.J. had constructed out of rock and unloaded our supplies at the edge of the water.

Surveying the house, I could see that it truly was as run down as they had described. It needed work from the bottom up. I made my way toward the front door with my load, thinking I would scout out my room.

"Hey," said E.J. behind me.

I turned to see him pointing with his thumb toward a small 8' x 4' structure.

"That's where we're staying, in the goat house."

I studied his face to see if he was being serious. He was. He walked over to the small brick structure, and entered. Shortly after, he popped his head out from the doorway.

"It's just for a couple of days. When Judd comes, it'll just be the two of you, easier for two than for three. "

I blinked at him, glued to my spot and eyeing the small structure. Surely he didn't mean all three of us were going to stay in there!

"Don't worry, the goats have moved out," he grinned.

We spent the rest of the day exploring the coffee plantation and planning out our course of action on the main house. It needed a new roof, new plaster, window frames, and just about everything else a house needs to operate. E.J. explained to me that we would be installing electric wiring and plumbing for when they could eventually get running water to the house. When Judd arrived in three weeks, he would be able to lend a hand. With Judd's help, E.J. had no doubt that we could make significant progress in a relatively short amount of time. E.J., after all, had a ministry to build.

The Kiles took me all over the red-earthed pathways of the plantation. Lush gardens were everywhere alongside narrow, muddy waterways used for everything from laundry to sewer. The work at the coffee plantation was in full swing and I met dozens of people involved in the processing of the coffee. The women we met wore T-shirts and bright cloths wrapped around their bodies and scarves or wraps on their heads. Almost all of them had infants secured to their backs under the cloths. The men generally wore more muted colors, selected from the masses of clothes sent over second hand from America through The Salvation Army and frequently bearing incongruent English messages across their chests. Men could be spotted unwittingly wearing everything from muscle club shirts to pregnancy shirts to lesbian pride shirts. Someday in the distant future, archaeologists will be thankful for organizations such as The Salvation Army, who helped spread these T-shirts across the world. Thanks to them, researchers will be able to determine that the wearers of these shirts ran in the "Gramma's Marathon," thought themselves a "Foxy Lady," were bearing "Twins (double arrow pointing down)," or, in case of an off day, found it necessary to warn their fellow humans that "My estrogen is off. What's your excuse?" What archaeologists might not be able to explain is why these shirts, found halfway across the world from their closet of origin, might be worn by men!

Everywhere we went people were kind to us and greeted us with a warm smile and a soft handshake as the Kiles spoke to them in Swahili. The Kiles had spent most of their early missionary service in Congo where they spoke Swahili and French, so they only knew basic greetings in Kinyarwanda. Even so, it could not have been more obvious how loved the Kiles were. Some of the women grasped Tudy by the shoulders and leaned in to brush one side of her head, then the other. Tudy would fill me in on the details of their lives as we walked away.

"She and her husband have eight children and they live on the hill just at that edge of the plantation." or, "He came to the Bible school 5 years ago and is now the pastor of a small church nearby."

At the end of the day, we sat down to one of the meals Tudy had packed for us—rice and kidney beans and some fresh mango, banana and a fruit that tasted like a combination of the two called a pawpaw. After the long day in the bright sun, I was grateful for the nourishment.

When we were done, E.J. and I waded out into the lake to cool off.

"Just don't swallow it," he reminded me, swishing at the water with one of his hands. "It'll give you the runs."

I eyed the lake's surface suspiciously just as he splashed a wall of water toward my face. I dove under the surface to escape. I popped up soon after, sending a wall of water his way. He held his breath and sent another back at me. Soon we were in the middle of a full-fledged war. From the shore we could hear Tudy yelling at us.

"You two are a couple of fools," she scolded us over the noise we were making, "and I'm going to be the one taking care of you when you're bent over sick in bed with stomachache and fever. You've got to respect this water," she added while the two of us straightened up, "because I guarantee it won't respect you."

IN GOD'S HANDS NOW

APRIL 7, 1994
KIGALI, RWANDA

As I watched and listened, the soldiers continued down the street, stopping at certain houses on a list they carried. Tutsi houses, I realized then.

The previous years had been leading up to this. Not even a year before, we had awakened in the middle of the night to the sound of crackling and loud pops. Seeing the glow through the window, we raced outside to see that the small kitchen building behind the house across the street from us was ablaze. Looking up and down the street and not seeing anybody racing to put it out, we sensed that something was not quite right. If it had been a normal cooking fire, people would have been lending a hand to help extinguish it. Instead, there was no sign of movement anywhere on the street. People remained indoors, hiding.

Attacks like this had been happening over the past few years more and more frequently. The worst was that there was nothing you could do. As far as anybody could tell, the people who had set the fire were lying in wait for the right people to react. Making a move to intervene would likely have been a deadly decision.

And now, something far worse was happening. As far as the men doing the killing were concerned, their Tutsi neighbors were in league with the Tutsi RPF army that had allegedly killed their Hutu president and was attacking their way of life. It did not matter that it was questionable who had *actually* killed the president—whether it was the RPF or the government army aligned Hutus opposed to the peace negotiations and looking for an excuse to trigger the "cleansing" of their nation—the result of the action was that people were afraid of the very people with whom they worked, went to church and even shared a table. All Tutsis were to be eradicated. There were to be no survivors. A Hutu card-bearing family was the only salvation. If there was a Tutsi among them sheltered within the household or married to a Hutu, all were likely to be killed. Man, woman or child—it did not matter.

With the sound of gunfire and explosions in my ears, I made my way back up to the house and through the front door. I was grateful to see Melanie's back as I passed the kitchen where she was preparing a pot of coffee. In our bedroom at the back of the house, I closed the door behind me and picked up the phone. When an official from the American Embassy answered, I spoke quietly into the receiver. I had spoken to her several times before and knew she was second or third in command. I told her what I had seen.

"Are you sure?" she asked. "Are you sure they are killing Tutsis?"

"They are going into Tutsi homes, firing shots and then blowing up the houses with a grenade as they leave. You tell me."

She paused, the sound of another explosion from the other end of the street filling the silence on the other end of the line.

"Well, we haven't heard any other reports of actual killing."

"Listen, I just saw them do it with my own eyes! They're still doing it!"

"Well, get your bags ready in case you have to be evacuated, and let us know if you see anything else."

I hung up and leaned back on the bed. Checking the door to make sure it was still closed I picked the phone back up and dialed the UN.

"Please," I told the official at the other end. "You need to send troops now. People are dying as we speak."

There was the same uncomfortable pause I had just experienced with the US Embassy, the same denial and the inability to comprehend that people were being killed. I repeated what I had seen. I held my phone out so that they could hear the gunfire for themselves. Finally, he sighed into the phone.

"Listen, there's nothing we can do. And frankly, we're confined to our barracks. We're not allowed to go out at all."

I replaced the phone on the cradle and pressed my temples. In the kitchen, Melanie moved plates around. Removed toast from the toaster.

IN GOD'S HANDS NOW

Out on the street, there was nothing, no sound from any living person at all. No screams. No talking. There was only the sporadic rat-tat-tat of the AK 47— a pause, an explosion, more gunfire.

Slowly, I walked to the kitchen. Melanie handed me some coffee and a piece of bread. Neither of us was hungry.

"Sit down," she said gently. "Eat something. We're going to need our strength."

She held my gaze for several seconds. I didn't know what to tell her about what I had seen. As it turned out, I didn't have to. By the look in her eyes, I could see that she already knew.

The day wore on. A deathly stillness had fallen over the streets of Kigali. The men who had been working their way down our street with guns and grenades had left, on to another neighborhood. Occasionally in the distance, we would hear the muffled sound of a semi-automatic weapon or the low boom of an explosion, and then nothing.

"I'm going to call Laurie," Melanie announced, placing her plate near the sink and abandoning the kitchen clean-up for later. Laurie Scheer was one of the missionaries who served with us. She and her husband Gary were the reason Melanie was here in the first place. Melanie had come to Rwanda to teach the Scheer's children. While Laurie had thought of her almost like a daughter at the beginning, she and Laurie had quickly developed into close friends.

I hung back in the kitchen, realizing suddenly that I was impatient to use the phone, as well. We needed to check in with our colleagues and friends. Word needed to be sent back home to our headquarters in Wheaton, Illinois about what was happening. It was still Wednesday night back home in the States. People would be finishing up weekly prayer meetings. If I could get word to them, maybe we could get some people praying on behalf of the people of Rwanda—on behalf of all of us.

While Melanie was wrapping up her phone call with Laurie, I prepared a fax to go to headquarters.

"We are in a bad way," I wrote, "Please pray."

The minute Melanie hung up the phone, I hit send on the fax machine.

She updated me on the Scheer's situation. "Well, they're all right," said Melanie. "They haven't seen what we saw on our street."

I wondered what Melanie had actually seen while I was out looking over the wall. She did not say anything and I did not ask. Images of the men casually tossing a grenade through the front door of our neighbor's home replayed in my mind.

Melanie. I was suddenly flooded with the urge to protect her, at all costs! I had waited so long for her. She was truly a gift from God. The idea that she was trapped in this scene with me filled me with a jolt of agony. As quickly as the thought came, another one just as startling occurred to me: What can I actually do?

Melanie seemed to sense what I was wrestling with. "It's in God's hands now," she said. She had said it with strength in her soft, high voice, but I did not miss the slight quiver to her lip. Her hands fell limply in her lap.

I took her in my arms and held her tight, squeezing her trim, athletic frame close. How I had been so blessed to have found her was beyond me.

"I love you," I whispered in her ear, allowing her short, curly brown hair to caress my cheek.

"And you know I love you," she said, her whole body relaxing as she said it, "No matter what happens."

"No matter what happens, it's all in His hands," I repeated.

We were interrupted by the sound of an engine on the street. Looking out the window, we watched as an army convoy arrived. There were several trucks, each filled with armed men. We recognized their uniforms. They were from the Rwandan government army. They stopped at the property next to ours, a lot which had been empty since we had moved in, and began to unload. There were dozens of men, all bearing rifles and various boxes. We watched as they unloaded a short canon, resting it on a bipod in the street for a few minutes, before hauling it off somewhere out of our view on the other side of our wall.

"Dear Lord," began Melanie beside me, but she trailed off. Just then, the phone rang. I picked it up.

"It's Dick," came a familiar voice at the other end of the line. It was my supervisor, Dick Jacobs, calling from Wheaton. They had received the fax. The secretary's husband was Jim Warren, an announcer with Moody Broadcasting, and had read it over the air. It was a relief to know that people were already praying for us half a world away.

"Can you guys get on a plane?" he wanted to know. WorldVenture does not take chances with their people in precarious political situations and was ready to evacuate us immediately.

"There aren't any planes. Nobody is moving at all except for military vehicles. I don't think we can even get to the airport right now," I told him after briefing him about what was happening. "There is too much going on in the streets."

Melanie left the room for a few minutes and I took the opportunity to explain a little bit about what I had seen.

"People are being killed all around us," I told him.

"Well, as soon as it's safe, we want you guys on a plane home. Understood? We're praying for—"

I waited for him to finish, but there was nothing.

"Hello? Hello?"

I hit the button on the phone several times, but there was not even a dial tone.

"What?" asked Melanie, swinging into view around the door frame.

"Phone's dead."

We stared at each other, wide-eyed. We were used to occasional phone outages, but this was different. Without communications, we were on our own in what was very quickly becoming a war zone.

"God's hands," she reminded me.

"God's hands," I repeated, allowing the thought to fill me with strength.

Next to us, the voices of men were beginning to fill the air. There was some gunfire in the distance. Not long after, we heard more gunfire, closer this time. It sounded like it was coming from up the hill, close to the Parliament Building, less than a kilometer away. It stopped. We waited. All of a sudden, the air was filled with a deafening noise. The soldiers beside us had starting firing. We ducked into the hallway away from all windows and pressed our hands over our ears. They kept firing and the air filled with the thunder of thousands of rounds.

"Get down," I yelled over the noise, pulling Melanie down onto the ground beside me. The floor in the hallway was cement, coated in a red paint. We lay flat, nose-to-nose, blinking at each other. Above us was the whistling sound of bullets.

"It'll be over soon," she mouthed, just as a thunderous boom filled the air and shook the house. The floor beneath us vibrated through our chests. They had fired a mortar. Several soft thumps landed on our tin roof as dirt and organic matter was displaced from the canon's discharge.

Suddenly, all went silent. We sat up, our pulses racing. Ducking as I walked, I went back into the office and picked up the phone. It was still dead. Desperate for news, I grabbed the radio from the bedroom. Gunfire from up the hill started back up then and I realized that they were shooting back at the soldiers next door to us. They fired a few rounds and stopped. Next to us, the storm reignited. We dove back onto the hall floor to wait it out, cringing in wait for the bullets that would take out our windows or our walls. When the noise died down once again, I ran around the house to see if there had been any damage. As far as I could tell, there was none, a small miracle in itself.

Realizing that this was going to continue for a while, we dragged a twin-sized mattress from one of the guest rooms into the hall to lie on. Over the radio, a man was reporting that the RPF had claimed the Parliament Building. He stated that the Tutsis had killed the Hutu president and were now attempting to take over the country. There were to be no Tutsis left alive. No man, woman or child who were of Tutsi origin. He called them "cockroaches that needed to be stamped out and destroyed."

The gunfire from next door started up again suddenly and without warning. This time, we lay on the mattress on our backs holding hands, breathing slowly and listening to the whistle overhead as thousands of pieces of metal ripped through the air above us faster than the speed of sound. The windows rattled when the mortars were fired, and we noted that more than one mortar was now in use. I was overcome at one point by the thought that I was no longer afraid, and I could see by the look on Melanie's face that she wasn't either. *What is wrong with me*, I wondered? There was no panic. No emotion, even. We were just going through the motions of what needed to be done to stay safe. We had detached and were now simply staring up at the ceiling waiting for it to pass.

When the shooting next door stopped again, we did not move for some time. The radio, beside us, had quit working during the latest exchange, and we knew then that the power was out. We had no way to find out what was happening. No way to find out if our friends were safe.

"In God's hands," I whispered without moving from my spot on the mattress. I was in a mild state of shock. Melanie, lying still beside me, squeezed my hand.

BANANA BREAD

1976
GISENYI, RWANDA

Once Judd arrived, we were able to make good progress on the house. Together, we stripped it of its roof, took out all of the old fixtures and windows, and scraped off all of the old plaster. The work was hard and the bright sun was relentless. At night, after we had cooled off in the lake, we lay in our cots in the old goat house and watched the rodents as they scurried between the roof and the wall. The goats may have moved out, but the rats had moved in!

On the weekends, we took the barge back to Gisenyi for a little pampering at the Kiles' house, letting Tudy cook for us, seemingly making something out of nothing from her sparse pantry. We would stay up late until 9 p.m.—what we call "missionary midnight" as it gets dark at 6 p.m. and light at 5:30 a.m. year round—and tell stories from our day and catch up on news from back home. My mother had stayed faithful with her letter writing and I eagerly pored over the handwritten notes she sent me. Mostly they were updates about how the family was doing, as well as news from the church and about the truck driving business. Her neat, looped handwriting conveyed that Dad was doing well and awaited my help at the end of my trip. I would read that about him and just shake my head. He was a good father, the best. But surely he understood that I had to make my own way. I was a man now and would make my own decisions. I had even started to grow a beard, something I knew he would never approve of.

The early mornings on those weekends in Gisenyi were relatively lazy, with Judd and me sleeping in as long as we dared. Judd is a gentle soul, with a kind smile and friendly word to say to everyone, and I was happy to be spending so much time with him. Eventually, the noise from the rest of the house would rouse us and we would eagerly head to the kitchen where we knew Tudy and her helper, Rosa, were preparing breakfast for us. After a week eating out of a cold box, we were eager for anything warm and fresh.

Throughout our time working on the house on the coffee plantation, people would float in and out, offering a hand where they could. Some of these people were there for the longer haul. Homer, for example, was an expert construction worker from California. From the beginning, he took me under his wing and taught me everything he knew about building and architecture. Older than I was by thirty years or so, he quickly became like a surrogate father to me in the absence of my own.

Others who were part of the missionary community were there for only short-term projects, though. One young man—I'll call him Don—was one of these: tall, handsome and from a privileged church in Tennessee. His father did carpentry as a hobby and had taught him well, so he was able to offer some skill toward the project. During the week he stayed with us out in the goat house, and accompanied us back on the weekend to receive the pampered treatment from Tudy Kile.

Saturday morning came early for us that particular weekend. We had stayed up late laughing and playing card games. There weren't too many other English speakers our age around, so when Don came to us three months into the project, we were admittedly a bit starved for social interaction. Tall, handsome and gregarious, Don had a magnetic personality. He was also a natural born leader and by his own admission was somewhat used to delegating. His family had been blessed, he explained. They had people who worked for them. Throughout the week he worked side by side with us, he remarked numerous times that it felt good to be applying himself to some hard work. "This is what it's all about," he said on the first Saturday morning of his stay, stretching toward the sun-filled sky as we three emerged from our room at the Kiles. The air was filled with the earthy scent of bread baking in the oven. We peeked into the kitchen. Tudy was hard at work over the sink, but Rosa saw us. She was dressed in a brown T-shirt and had a bright orange, red and white print cloth wrapped around her mid-section to the bottom of her ankles. On her head she wore a red floral wrap. She flung her hands at us and spoke to Judd in Kinyarwanda, her bright eyes flashing against skin the color of roasted coffee.

"Not yet," she told us. Don looked back and forth between them, smiling broadly.

"Is she your sister?" he asked Judd, to which Judd responded by a startled eye bulge.

"Does she look like my sister?" He laughed. Don laughed, too.

"Maybe in the ears," he joked. "I had to ask." He looked back over at Rosa who was watching them with a smirk from the stove. When he caught her eye, he held out his hand to her. "Mwaramutse."

"Ah!" cried Judd, his eyes crinkling with amusement as Rosa shook his hand, a smile hiding in the corner of her mouth. Even Tudy stopped scrubbing fruit with bleach water and turned around.

"Well now," she said. "Isn't that something?"

"He speaks Kinyarwanda!" Judd went on. "See, I told you, brother, you were born for the mission field."

"Nah," shrugged Don politely. "I only learned a few words. 'Good morning', 'thank you' and 'I need a doctor'."

"Well, that's already twice as many as Gary here," he laughed. I punched him lightly on the arm. I'd been working as hard as I could on learning, but after three months, the language wasn't coming as easily as I had hoped.

Since breakfast wasn't quite ready, we headed out the back door to stare at the lake, only a stone's toss off the back of the house. The surrounding trees were filled with the usual cacophony of birds announcing the morning.

"You're digging this, huh?" Judd asked Don with a smile. It was clear that Judd was proud of his home and the work they were doing. Nothing pleased him more than to be able to introduce it to visitors.

"Yeah, it's incredible. If this is what doing the Lord's work means, then sign me up," said Don. "It's good, honest work," he added, rubbing at the sore muscles in his shoulders.

"Is that right? You thinking of becoming a lifer?" asked Judd.

Don chuckled, "Oh, I don't know about that. My folks might never let me hear the end of it if I left home for good."

"*Ni byo*," I whispered. I understood that all too well.

"So, you do have some words hiding in there," said Judd to me with a wink. "Now that Don's here, you've got some competition."

I laughed good-naturedly and led the way out the door to the lake. We took a seat on the ground near the lake's edge to wait for breakfast. Meanwhile, Don took the opportunity to ply Judd with questions about Rosa.

"Forget it, man," Judd said jokingly to Don. "She's the coffee plantation manager's daughter. Besides she's not interested in *abazungu* (white person) like us. I think she's already engaged to a Rwandan."

Don laughed it off, but I could tell he was still thinking about her, and why not? She was pretty and a good Christian girl. But there was no way I was going to settle down with a Rwandan! Doing that would mean I was committed to possibly staying there the rest of my life as a missionary and that was something I was not even open to considering.

In fact, the discussion of dedicating one's entire life to the mission field was a common one amongst us. Obviously, Judd's family had done it. There were several others who lived near the Kiles in Gisenyi who had also chosen that life. Paul Okken, the older man I had flown over with had done it, too, returning from furlough with his wife on my first trip over. They had spent much of their life in Congo and had been recently moved by the mission headquarters to help work on the burgeoning Bible school there. Only a week or so prior, Paul had looked me in the eye while on the barge over to Cyimbili.

"Gary," he said, "did you know that 50% of short-term missionaries come back as career missionaries?"

"Paul, that's nice, but 50% don't," I told him with a smile.

He looked out over the lake as if he and the water were sharing a private joke.

"I'm not going to become a missionary," I shrugged. Paul only looked at me and smiled, but I shook my head. Sure, I was having fun and I enjoyed doing something that I felt God wanted me to do, but there was no way I was missionary material. I was a truck driver, a farmer and maybe even a builder—but not a preacher or a teacher or anything like that.

After a few minutes, Tudy popped her head out the door to tell us we could come and eat once we had washed up. A couple minutes later we were seated around their small dining table. Before us on the table were mounds of fresh fruit and, in the middle, a steaming loaf of banana bread.

"This looks fantastic," I told Tudy, who was busily making her way around the table and filling cups of coffee for us. E.J., too, had found his way back to the house after having been out already to lend a hand down the road. One of their neighbors had been working on their gate and needed a couple of tools. He sat at the head of the table.

"Well now, that's Rosa's bread you're looking at there," she said. "I can't take any credit for it."

We passed the loaf hungrily around the table, along with the plate filled with cut fruit and sugar for the coffee. When Rosa paused at the table, Don made another attempt to engage her.

"This is good," he said, pointing at the bread and giving her a thumbs-up sign. She nodded politely at him and said something to Judd, to which he responded with a chuckle. Not sure what the joke was, Don continued.

"No really, I didn't expect to find banana bread here."

Judd translated for his friend and Rosa shot back with something that made all three of the Kiles laugh.

"What?" asked Don, looking between them.

"She said, 'What? You did not expect to find bananas in the tropics?'" explained Judd.

Don laughed, his face flushing ever so slightly. "No, no – it makes sense. I can see that now."

Rosa looked directly at Don now, a look of mischief on her face. Judd translated for her again.

"And is it any good? Is it like your banana bread at home?"

"Oh yes! Definitely! It's different, though."

"She wants to know how," said Judd after explaining to her what he had said.

"Well, I don't know. It does taste different," he said, pointing at a small section of crust that had darkened to near black in the Kiles' charcoal oven. Maybe next time just don't cook it so long."

Judd exploded in laughter and Rosa's eyes grew large as Tudy told her what Don had said, shaking her head all the while. E.J. held his mouthful of food closed and took a couple of swats at his knee. Rosa gripped her stomach and collapsed to the floor she was laughing so hard.

"What?" asked Don, cautiously smiling, "What's so funny?"

"She thinks it's hilarious that you're trying to tell her how to cook a local specialty," explained Judd when he could speak.

"Now wait a minute, I didn't mean—" began Don, attempting to backtrack, but nobody could hear him over the laughter in the room. Rosa, still on the floor opposite Don behind the table could scarcely get her breath. Finally, after the laughter had died down, Rosa used the wall to get to her feet.

"Mwaramutse," she nodded at Don, her eyes still wet with laughter. "Good morning."

"What? You speak a little English?" He asked, wide-eyed.

"Only 'good morning', 'thank you' and 'I need a doctor,'" she answered before turning back to her duties.

From the kitchen, we could hear her still chuckling amongst the clanging pans. E.J., beside me at the table, let out a loud hoot.

BRINGING IN THE TENT

APRIL 8, 1994
KIGALI, RWANDA

We had left our tent outside.

I had not meant to linger near the window, but when I got up for a glass of water from the kitchen, I saw it out there waving in the air like a flag.

It had been muddy on a camping trip the previous weekend so Melanie and I had rinsed it out by hand and left it on the line to dry. That was five days ago. And now it was starting to rain.

"What are you doing?" asked Melanie from the hallway when I didn't come back right away. Her voice did not convey worry so much as it did curiosity.

"Oh…nothing."

I walked back into the hall corridor where we had been for the bulk of the previous 24 hours. We had tried to sleep in our own bed, but were awakened in the middle of the night by more gunfire, so we ended up back in the hallway and stayed put. With the exception of the occasional breaks, the fighting outside showed no signs of letting up. We were exhausted, numb and vaguely aware that it was now Friday morning.

Melanie put down a book she was trying to distract herself with and looked up at me.

"It's that tent out there. It's starting to rain," I explained, somewhat distantly.

She brought her knees up to her chest and leaned her head back against the wall, studying me through her dark frames. I knew that look.

"It's a good tent. I don't want it to get wrecked."

Slowly, she picked her up her book and found where she had left off. Taking that as a sign of permission—or at least of no resistance—I walked back down the hallway toward the window and listened. Next to us, I could hear the soldiers talking, but for the moment, nobody was shooting.

We were in a lull.

Outside, the rain was picking up. I watched as the fabric of the tent began to take on large splotches of water. If I hurried I could bring it inside before it got too wet. I hated the thought of having to leave it out to dry again for several more days. It's not easy to dry things outside during the rainy season, least of all tent fabric. If we left it out during another deluge, it would just be dirty all over again and the fabric would be rough.

It had been an exhausting 24 hours. Every time the soldiers next to us let loose, Melanie and I lay flat on the mattress next to each other until it passed. We listened as the bullets whistled overhead and as dirt clods from the mortars hit our humble tin roof. During these times, we did not attempt to speak over the noise. I do not remember if we even prayed, although I am certain we must have, at the very least silently. We just lay still, and waited.

After the two armies had exchanged fire several times, there would be a break. If it was daytime, we would get up, check on the house, grab a bite to eat, make sure the dog was OK, and then flop back down on the hallway mattress. If it was during the night, we would simply exhale when the fighting stopped and attempt to go back to sleep.

When the gunfire had first started early on Thursday, Melanie asked me to go talk to our night guard and offer him an outside room so that he would not have to be in the open, caught in a potential rain of bullets. Normally, he spent the night outside manning the gate, but today he readily accepted the confinement of walls and a door in exchange for not having to maneuver the streets. During the breaks in fire, he went over to the wall and gathered news from other Hutu neighbors. Some of them believed that the army was actually positioned closer to us down the hill and were firing from a nearby school. He relayed this information quietly to me through the door before resuming his reinforced post in the room. Eventually, the thunder of a mortar would shake the house and rattle the windows and we would take our position once again in the hallway, lying low on the mattress for safety as bullets tore through the damp air above us.

BRINGING IN THE TENT

After a while, the storm would subside and we would peek from windows in an attempt to figure out what was happening around us.

It was during one of these times when I noticed the truck. It had been abandoned on a hill across the valley from us on a main road and remained there for part of the day. Curious, I kept an eye on it, wondering why it was stopped there. It wasn't until many hours later that I figured out its purpose.

Watching through my window, I noticed an army vehicle slow down as it approached the parked truck from behind and come to a stop. Men emerged from the army vehicle and walked up to the first vehicle. They opened the tailgate and immediately began unloading boxes from it.

At first I wasn't sure what it was, and then I realized that it was beer. Boxes and boxes of Primus beer—so much it took nearly an hour to unload it all and transfer it to the army vehicle. I watched them as they did it, puzzling all the while at the prioritization of such an occupation in the middle of a war zone. It was not until later that I would hear rumors that beer and drugs were what the Interahamwe killing mobs were given to keep them in a state in which they could continue to lift knives and spiked clubs against their neighbors, a state in which they would remain for nearly 100 days straight.

But I could not have known any of that then. On Day 2, late Friday morning, I was still trying only to figure out what was going on. To get my bearings and get done what needed to be done. But what needed to be done? What *could* be done?

Staring out into the yard where the tent was darkening in the rain, I thought about my colleagues and friends, spread out across the city and country. The Scheers. The Bjorklunds. The Muellers. Were they experiencing the same thing we were? Was there heavy fire like this all over Rwanda? Many of my Rwandan brothers at the Bible school and at the vocational school there were Tutsi. Were they safe? What about Alexi, the pastor I had been mentoring? He and his family were Hutu, sure, but certainly this did not guarantee their safety. And Tudy Kile—what of her? There was no way to know.

My heart was heavy when I thought about the Mueller family. They had only been there for nine months as missionaries and were still learning the language. To make matters worse, they had two small children with them, a little boy and a girl.

Please God, I prayed. *Please.*

A surge of water from the sky slapped the windowpane and I couldn't stand it anymore. Slipping on a pair of shoes, I went and took down the tent before it became soaked. While I folded it, I paused to listen to the soldiers speaking in low voices from the other side of the wall. There was the clink of metal on metal —a mortar being loaded in its tube.

Realizing my precarious position, I gathered up the rest of the tent in my arms and made for the door, closing it too hard behind me. I stood frozen, my heart beating desperately in my throat.

"Is that you?" called Melanie from the hall, just as an explosion from next door shook the entire house, vibrating the ground through my feet. I rounded the corner into the hallway where she lay on her side, propped up on an elbow watching for me.

"The tent's inside," I said briskly, evenly, not able to meet her eyes. "It's safe."

Outside our home, the sky filled with smoke and water and the thunderous echo of war.

THE BEARD

1976
WINDOM, MN

"Well, that thing's coming off."

I was home now, back in Minnesota. My entire family had met me at the airport. My dad was especially pleased to see me. From my mother's letters, I knew that he had been eagerly awaiting my return so that he could get my help with his trucking business. I was glad to lend him a hand and grateful to have a job waiting for me, but I was also aware that in the nine months I had spent on Lake Kivu something had changed in me. On my own, I had learned to take care of myself and to make decisions using the head God had given me. I had been given the chance to be in charge of my own destiny and I had thrived. In short, I had grown up. And if anybody doubted it, they could look at my face and it was as plain as day. I had grown a beard, a beard that my father was now focused in on like a hive of bees on a home-wrecking bear.

"What..this?"

I reached up and tugged at the reddish blond crop on my chin and flashed him a grin.

He shook his head and sniffed.

I looked off to the side and tossed my suitcase into the trunk of the car. I had known he would be upset about the beard, of course. There was a little part of me that had even hoped he would be. In a small way, it represented how I felt now. I was me, not him. I was capable of my own decisions. I was also enjoying showing it off to my brothers and sister.

"You keeping that?" He asked once we were inside the car. I smiled enigmatically and looked out the window as if to imply that I just might.

"What was it like?" asked my sister Carol, sitting next to me.

"Warm and sunny," I said, "like it was always springtime. We swam in the lake a lot."

"Did they make you eat bugs?" asked Brian. Brian is one of the twins. He and Bruce are the youngest in my family.

"Nobody *made* me," I said mysteriously, bouncing my eyebrows at him. They giggled uproariously.

"What do you miss most about home, Fritz?" Randy asked, calling me by my nickname. I looked out over the landscape ahead of us. It seemed so strange to be riding so smoothly.

"Paved roads," I said, to which they all laughed.

"That's my boy," said my Dad quietly, choking up proudly.

That night around the dinner table, I looked at the faces of my family. My four brothers and sister bantered per usual, as if I had never left. My mother, strong and capable, pulled out a fresh loaf of bread from the oven and set it on the table next to the roast, surrounded by steaming piles of potatoes and carrots. At the head of the table, my father sat quietly listening to the chatter. When I caught his eye, he winked at me.

"Why don't you start us off, son," he said, peering at me fondly from across the table. I smiled, bowed my head, and started the prayer. After I was finished, each sibling took his or her turn before my mother and father finished the blessing.

When we were done, there was an uncustomary silence around the table. I looked up at my father who was so happy to have me home. I knew he expected me to help him build his company—his little trucking empire—and I could see that he needed the help. He looked tired. I was glad to lend him a hand. But it would be on my terms now. I knew that I had a passion for agriculture and I wanted to put it to use. I knew that I wanted to go back to school and finish up there, too. Maybe even take some classes that would help me out with that endeavor. Maybe I would even start up my own farm someday. Whatever the case, I had my own plans and my own life to lead.

Even so, it felt good to be back with my family. They had been my anchor all of my life and they were genuinely happy to have me back.

THE BEARD

My brothers had teased me about the beard, of course, but I couldn't help feeling a bit of pride about it—even though I knew very well that now that I was home it wouldn't last long. It had served its purpose and I was done with it.

"It's good to be home," I said, looking around the table at their smiling, healthy faces.

And I meant it. Like I said, I now had the confidence of knowing that I had my own plans and my own life to lead.

Or so I thought.

REFUGE

APRIL 8, 1994
KIGALI, RWANDA

We were sitting shoulder to shoulder on the mattress in the hallway when a loud, rapid banging on the metal gate in front of the house took us by surprise. Melanie and I looked at each other. Was it the Embassy? Had they finally sent someone to come get us?

Melanie dove into the bathroom to prepare herself for a potential journey while I jogged to the window. Our night guard, a twenty-two- year-old Rwandan man named Justin, was opening the gate. I watched as he leaned out to speak to whoever it was on the other side. My mind raced through the contents of the bag I had packed. Had I remembered to put in my passport? We knew they would be coming, but now that somebody was actually at our door, I felt totally unprepared. I began haphazardly straightening papers on my desk.

After a few minutes, there was a soft knocking at the front of our house and a male voice called up.

"It is a woman with three children. They live down the street," said Justin in Kinyarwanda.

"Yes?" I asked, unable to understand what he was getting at. What did a woman and her children have to do with the US Embassy?

"They wish to take refuge with you."

I stopped shuffling stacks of papers and stared at the wood grain on the desk. I had made that desk myself, back in Gisenyi. I thought back to the soft strokes I had used to coat it with clear varnish. I reached down and touched it. My life in Gisenyi was several years behind me now.

"Of course," I called down, without leaving the office. Already, Melanie was heading down to meet them.

"Yes, please tell them to come in," she instructed him, her voice calm despite the stress of the previous days.

When I heard voices at the door, I went down to join them just as Melanie was leading them inside the house.

"You're safe here," Melanie reassured the woman and her children. Only the woman spoke, and only barely above a whisper to answer "yes" or "no" to direct questions or to repeat the word, "Murakoze," *thank you*, over and over.

"You must be hungry," she told them, leading them toward the kitchen. "I will make you something to eat."

"Please, no," the woman said distantly before trailing off. Catching herself staring at a plaque on our wall, she nervously glanced between us before finally looking down again, resting on the head of a small child in front of her. I looked over at the plaque she was looking at. It was the one that said *Great strength comes from faith in God*. I tore my own gaze away from it and studied her.

She was dressed simply in a knit shirt with a brown cloth wrapped around her mid-section and legs. She wore a brown and green cotton scarf on her head. The children, two girls and a boy, ranged between the ages of three and seven.

Melanie and I exchanged glances from across the hallway.

"Will you show them to the guest room?" she asked me in English. "I'll go make some…some rice."

I could sense her hesitation. In Rwanda it is customary to offer guests the very best food that is in the house. Since the fighting had begun, we had no way to get to the market at the end of the street for fresh fruits or vegetables and had fairly well exhausted our own supply at that point. Luckily, because of the nature of life in Kigali over the previous years, we had always taken care to make sure that we had extra food stores on hand in case the markets closed down and we had no way to get supplies. At the time the president's plane was shot down, we had nearly a hundred pounds of rice in our stores, as well as some frozen meat. And that was about it.

"Good choice," I told her with a smile. Her shoulders relaxed and she made for the kitchen.

I smiled warmly at the woman and her children and led them down the hallway past our mattress, which took up most of the floor space. They did not ask about it and I did not feel compelled to explain it. When we got to the room they could stay in, I held out a hand.

"Please, be comfortable here. You are safe here."

The four of them shuffled in, the woman directing two of the younger kids by the shoulder as they walked. In the room were a double bed and two twins covered in patchwork quilts. There would be space for them there. She nodded at me once and I left.

In the kitchen, I found Melanie bent over the stove, pouring rice into a large pan.

"Do you know them?" I asked her, "The children?"

She shook her head.

"I may have seen them before. They look somewhat familiar. Whatever the case, they look scared stiff. Did you see the little boy's eyes?"

"But they are," I dropped my voice, "shorts," not daring to use the word "Hutu" lest they overhear us. During the previous four years, we had been forced to reshape the way we spoke of people. Hutus had become "shorts" and Tutsis had become "talls," whereas before 1990, we barely even noticed or registered the difference between the two ethnic groups at all. So much had changed in four years.

"Maybe they are, maybe they are not. Maybe not fully shorts, anyway. We don't know about the father." She paused. Neither of us wanted to think about the possibilities that may have driven them to our doorstep.

"What they must have seen," said Melanie shaking her head. She began filling the pan with water from our reserves. Our faucets had run dry by then, as well. "It's good they're here. They're safer here than out there."

I nodded, feeling that what she said must be true, although I had no idea why. Is it because we are Americans? Is it because we are white? It hardly felt fair. At the same time, I was well aware that the fight going on outside was internal. It was the equivalent to civil war. We were not the target. Even as I thought it, I felt flooded with a wave of guilt. Our Rwandese friends were out there somewhere. How were they faring? What of our Tutsi friends and colleagues?

Revived somewhat from the addition of people into our household, we talked about the situation with renewed vigor in the kitchen while we waited for the rice to be done. If only we could listen to the radio again and find out what was happening in the city, we might know whether it was safe to chance a break for the embassy or even to the airport. Based on what we had seen already, though, we feared it would be a suicide mission. One of our colleagues had been shot just a year or so before, after all. He was out driving when he encountered a group of armed men who opened fire on him when he turned around to go the other way. His father, in the passenger seat, was shot in the leg while he was shot in the hand that was on the stick shift. He and his family had no other choice but to leave so that he could have emergency surgery on his hand. There was no reason to believe that the same—or worse—wouldn't happen given the current situation. Every way we looked at it, it seemed like the best option to just stay put. That is, of course, unless things became even more out of control next door.

There had been no activity from the soldiers in the lot next to ours for at least an hour and we were anticipating that it would begin again at any time. I sat at the table and Melanie rubbed my shoulders, which I had not even realized were in knots from the stress and from camping out on a mattress on and off for thirty-six hours. Even while there was a battle going on literally next door to us, she was taking care of me. After a while, I reached up and took one of her hands and leaned my cheek to it.

When the rice was done, Melanie dished out some large scoops into bowls and placed them on a tray.

"Would you?" she asked, blinking sweetly at me.

She was attempting playful, but the strain behind it was not lost on me. I took the tray from her, realizing that she wanted to clean up before the next round of fire began. Since it had been nearly an hour now since we had heard anything, it was due.

Thinking I would drop off the food and return to help her, I walked briskly down the hall toward the guest room, balancing the bowls of rice carefully lest they fall and make a mess. With water limited as it was, a food mess was the last thing we needed.

I reached the room and knocked softly on the door. There was no answer. I tried knocking again, still nothing.

"Hello?" I asked into the room. When there was no response, I turned the handle on the door and pushed it open slowly. The room was empty.

"Hello?" I called again, setting down the tray full of rice on a table across the room. I walked down the hallway and peeked into the darkened bathroom. There was nobody there.

"Melanie? Are they down there with you?" I called through the living room toward the kitchen.

"Who?" she answered back.

A feeling of panic was rising inside of me. I crossed through the living room to the front door and pulled it open. Our guard was in the driveway, near the gate.

"Did they come out here?" I called to him.

"Who? The family?" he responded.

"Yes," I answered, but I could see by his expression that they had not. I went back inside. Had they managed to leave the property without anybody seeing? It seemed unlikely. Worse, had somebody managed to get on the property and take them? Where were they? Were they still here?

Driven now by the thought that there may be people on my property without my permission, I picked up my pace. My senses alert, I scanned the yard and the gate around it. When I saw no movement, I raced back inside. Melanie. Where was Melanie?

"Gary?" She asked from the kitchen doorway through the dining room. "Is everything OK?"

"I don't know yet," I answered, relieved that she was still safe. Even so, my eyes continued to race around the room for our guests. I was looking for a sign—some sort of clue as to what had happened. Where were they? I looked behind the futon on the other side of the room.

Confused, I decided to retrace my steps. I walked briskly back down to their room and stopped in the doorway, listening. On a whim, I dropped to the floor on my hands and knees and peered under the bed. Four sets of eyes stared back at me. A shock ran through me. I sat up. A realization of how desperate the situation really was began to settle over me.

THE CALL

1977
WINDOM, MN

Rwanda and I have a relationship built on returns and recalls. I leave and she calls me back. It is a pattern, set from the very beginning.

I had not taken the right classes in the right order to receive my one year Bible Certificate, so I resumed my studies at Northwestern for a couple of quarters. I quickly fell back into helping my dad out with his routes, driving refrigerated meat back and forth between southern Minnesota and Chicago in the dark blue cabover Freightliner I was constantly working over with more chrome and more lights. I decided at that point to enroll at South Dakota State University where I could take other classes I was interested in—particularly in agriculture. I enrolled for the fall semester and loved it. Since it is a secular university, I was forced to live my faith and found myself growing with the challenge. When I was finished there, I was eager to get into farming. Unfortunately, our family didn't have the kind of land I needed, so once again, I ended up driving trucks full time.

After a year on the road, something interesting happened. I was struck with a thought, an idea, an itch, really. I was on I-90 in southern Minnesota when it happened. It was right around mile marker 236.

What am I doing with my life? I wondered. And then, as the thought drilled itself under my skin and spread along my veins, I asked it again.

"What am I doing?" I asked out loud, pounding the steering wheel for emphasis.

It was 5 a.m. and I was heading back from Chicago, having just dropped my cargo and quickly finding a backload. It was just me and the Lord in that cab.

Just then, I was hit rapid fire with Matthew 6:33 where it says, "Seek ye first the kingdom of God and his righteousness and all these things shall be added unto you."

I returned to the question. So, what was I doing with my life? My answer was simple:

Well, I'm basically doing what I want to do, I'm out here making money and that's my whole goal—making money. Well, and making my truck sparkle.

I was lonely, too. Sure, I was still young, but it was always in the back of my mind that I wanted to find somebody to love and to settle down with. I was looking for a good solid girl who loved God like I did, somebody who took care of herself and who needed me. Somebody who I could love back and maybe even raise some children with.

Well, Lord, I said, *bring me the right person and I'll do just that. I've been faithful to you.*

But was that enough? Was that what I was supposed to do in life—settle down with a wife, drive a sharp, shiny truck…and just make money?

That next Wednesday night, I was heading back from Chicago. I had hauled refrigerated meat into the windy city and was now hauling a load of groceries for Nash Finch Company to Sioux Falls, South Dakota. It just so happened that I was near the town of Luverne, where one of the missionaries I had known in Rwanda was going to be speaking at the local church. I decided to go.

After the service at First Baptist, I went over to the home where Glen and Kathy Kendall were staying to do some catching up. They were back on their home visit and were doing the rounds missionaries have to do in order to gain support from the churches. They looked happy and we recounted stories from my visit well into the night over glasses of iced tea.

"You know, we could really use your help back over there," Glen told me across the living room table. "We've just started another building project and could use another skilled set of hands."

I shifted uncomfortably on the sofa and took a sip of tea from my glass.

THE CALL

"Yeah, well, I wish I had the money," I said, as my life literally flashed before my eyes. There were the trucks and...what about my dream to become a farmer? And while the thought was barely clear in my mind, I remembered all too well the options for dating in Rwanda, little to nil. I reached out and set my glass of ice tea on the table in front of me, focusing on the beads of condensation as they absorbed into the coaster.

"Well, you should think about it," Kathy chimed in. "I know Tudy sure would be happy to see you. We all would be."

"I know E.J. would love your help. He's out there building a hydroelectric plant, you know." Glen chuckled lightly. We all knew how E.J. could be when he got going on a project. On weekends, when I had stayed with them, I remember all too well hearing him walking around in the middle of the night. He would go to bed for a little while, and then get up and work by the light of a kerosene lamp until the wee hours of the morning. Then he would go to bed again and still be up before anyone else.

"A hydroelectric plant, huh?" I smiled at the thought. If anyone could do it, he could.

"Yes, to get electricity to the Bible school, that needs building, too."

My conversation with God on the highway played out in my mind and I let out a deep sigh.

"I'll think about it," I said.

It was late, so I thanked them for their hospitality and excused myself. I did still have a truck full of groceries that needed unloading, after all. When I got to the Nash Finch warehouse most of the night was finished. I unloaded the groceries but I couldn't stop thinking about mile marker 236 and the conversation with the Kendalls. When I got back to the farmhouse in Windom, it was the middle of the afternoon and all was uncharacteristically quiet. I went out into the living room to sit for a minute with a glass of ice water. Next to me was an end table filled with stacks of magazines and scribbled notes. That's when I saw the letter. It was from Rwanda. I picked it up and opened it.

"Gary, we'd really like you to consider coming back out and helping us to build here in Cymbili," wrote Paul Okken.

I thought back to the conversation Paul and I had had back on the barge months before.

"Fifty-percent of short-term missionaries come back as career missionaries," he had said. His voice haunted me still.

I flopped down on the couch and looked around at the simply decorated farm style living room. In the afternoon lighting, the earth tones of the fabric seemed even darker. My eyes settled on my father's empty recliner and I sighed deeply.

Reluctantly conceding that God must be speaking to me, I decided to mention it to my pastor that next Sunday. It was the least I could do under the circumstances.

"But I really don't have the money for plane tickets and the monthly support," I told him, somewhat weakly. That was a good reason, right?

Wrong. Within a matter of weeks, the members of the church had scraped together the funds for me to go back over. I was out of excuses. And so...I went back.

PREPARATIONS

APRIL 8, 1994
KIGALI, RWANDA

"Whoa," I said, taking a breath and allowing the adrenalin to settle within me. I leaned back down and peered under the bed where the eyes still blinked at me. I showed them my empty hands.

"It's OK," I told them. "I'm not going to hurt you. Nobody's going to hurt you here."

I could hear the youngest whimpering slightly, pressing further into his mother's side. He had recoiled from me when he saw that my eyes were on him.

I reached up slowly and took one of the bowls of rice off the tray. I held it close to the ground so they could see it. The woman looked from the rice back up to my face uncertainly.

"My wife thought you might like something to eat."

The woman under the bed stared back at me, the whites of her eyes contrasted against her dark skin. I could see it then. Whatever it was she had just lived through, it had been bad. She nodded once, slowly, and dropped her eyes.

"OK," I said.

I stood to my feet, my knees cracking and popping as I straightened. I was used to activity. Being holed up in the house while a battle raged outside was wearing on me more than just mentally. I wanted to do something – not just sit back and wait while people were being slaughtered around me. For the first time since Thursday morning, the shock had cleared enough for me to actually register what was going on around me. I was starting to feel.

One of the children, a girl, began to wiggle her way out from under the bed at her mother's encouragement. I watched her, her shoulders and back bowing as she reached for some leverage to pull herself out. Like most Rwandese children, she wore her hair cropped close to discourage lice in the tropical climate. I noticed then for the first time she wore a simple light blue blouse and navy skirt, a school uniform.

Why she had chosen that particular outfit on a day that there was clearly going to be no school was beyond me. Maybe it had been wishful thinking. Or maybe it was all she had to wear. Close behind her, her older brother shimmied his way out and I noticed that he, too, wore his school uniform—a blue shirt and navy pants. The youngest, too young to be in school, wore a simple T-shirt and a pair of shorts a couple of sizes too big for him. The three stood in a close cluster and watched me cautiously as their mother squeezed her way out from under the bed. A small wooden cross on a dark string peeked out from the neckline of the girl's blouse and I was suddenly overcome with this family's plight. For all I knew, they weren't wearing their uniforms because they were hoping for school against all odds that day. Perhaps they were wearing their uniforms because they had not yet had a chance to change out of them.

The thought shot through me like a bolt.

Here was a family, too scared to even return to their own home. What had happened there? What had they seen?

I fought down a sore spot in my throat. How could this be happening? I wanted to yell. I wanted to stomp and rage. These were God's children, all of us, God's children!

"Excuse me, I..." I stopped. There was nothing to say. Realizing then that my fists had clenched into balls, I stretched my fingers deliberately open, took a deep breath, and left the room.

* * *

That night, Melanie and I drifted through dreams of peaceful tree-lined waters, of the house we had yet to buy together, of the children we had yet to hold. When the gunfire began again, punctuating the silence and ripping holes in our sails, we lay wide-eyed in the dark waiting for nothing and everything all at once. With fingers interlocked, we exhaled our shallow breaths into prayers for our loved ones and waited through the whistling of bullets overhead and the thump of mud clots and plant matter as they hit the metal roof. Eventually, the storm of bullets died down and we were encompassed once again by the silence that lay moored across Rwanda like a fog.

In the morning, when the light was just a dim glow from the windows, Melanie rose early and went down to the kitchen in order to make breakfast. I could hear her working in there, pouring rice into a pot and starting the stove. I sat up and listened for signs of life from the guest room. Aside from the occasional heavy night breath of children, there had been nothing from them all night. I crept down the hall and peered out the window in our bedroom. The sun was creeping up over the horizon casting orange on the trees in our yard. I listened for birds, dogs, and people — but there was nothing. No sound at all.

I headed to the bathroom to brush my hair and teeth, dropping my toothpaste and brushes back in my travel bag when I was done. There was no need to get dressed. I had slept in my clothes.

It was close to 9 a.m. when we heard someone banging on the metal gate again. We were all in the kitchen, where Melanie had served our guests the humble breakfast of the rice she had prepared and some tea. Melanie and I looked at each other while the mother of the three small children leapt to her feet and ushered her children toward the guest room. After a few moments, Justin came up the sloped driveway and told us that there were soldiers down there and that they wanted to speak with me. I followed after him.

There were three of them, dressed in camouflage and dirty from the previous days spent in smoke and mud and makeshift barracks.

"Look," began the man in the middle, adjusting his cap, "we are bringing in some heavy artillery. You need to get out of here." He wore an AK-47 strapped across his chest. I noticed then that they all wore AK-47s strapped to their chests.

I nodded, not about to argue.

"Are the roads open?" I asked.

The man sniffed and looked around while one of his companions lit a cigarette. He pointed off down the street.

"Follow that road down the hill and through the valley, go past the swamp and follow it around the way. That's how we're getting our supplies in. You should be able to get into the main part of town that way."

I knew the road he meant. The only problem was, I wasn't quite sure what we were supposed to do once we got into town.

"But where in the world are we going to go?" I asked him. The soldier smoking the cigarette tapped some ash onto the ground.

"Why don't you go to your American Embassy?" he said, shrugging.

I told them I would consider it and went inside to tell Melanie what he had said. I found her in the kitchen wiping out the dishes we had used for breakfast with a cloth. She watched me tentatively from the sink.

She broke the tension with a joke. "I hope you told them they can't use the bathroom here," she said.

I sniffed a stifled laugh. She knew as well as I did that they couldn't care less about using our bathroom! I pulled out a chair at the kitchen table for her.

"I think we should talk."

She narrowed her eyes at me before crossing the floor to where I was standing. She sat down.

"They said they are about to bring in some heavy artillery, the big guns, so to speak."

She gave me a look. "Well, those haven't exactly been BB guns they've been shooting over there!"

"Exactly! Which means this is about to get ugly."

"-er," she added. "Ugli*er*."

We both sat there for a few minutes without speaking.

"Where will we go?" she asked finally. I explained to her the route the soldier had told me to take and that he had suggested we go to the US Embassy.

"I don't know," she said. "How do we know we shouldn't just stay put?"

"Melanie," I interrupted, "I don't think he was asking. They want us out of here."

"This could be really bad," she said, her eyes suddenly drained of hope. "We don't have a clue about what's going on out there."

"The soldier said that we would be safe to go that way," I reminded her, wondering at my own use of the word "safe." "God's hands, remember?"

PREPARATIONS

I reached across the table and took her hand. She exhaled nervously before looking up at me with a half-smile.

"You're right."

We bowed our heads right then and said a simple prayer, asking God for guidance and safety. When we were done, we felt better about the decision to go. We stood to go get our things and noticed then that the woman we had taken in was standing in the kitchen doorway. From the look on her face, we could see that she understood enough about what was going on.

"Please," she said in Kinyarwanda, "We want to go with you."

Without hesitation, Melanie walked over to her and placed a hand on her shoulder.

"We are leaving soon. Will you be ready to go in 15 minutes?"

She turned to collect her children as Melanie looked back over at me. I nodded. Of course we would take her.

We began a quick sweep of the house, going from room to room to make sure we weren't leaving anything important behind or out in the open. I put more electronics with the computer in the attic, along with some of our important papers. Spying the tent I had brought inside the day before, I snatched it up and stuffed it into the attic, as well. If somebody broke into our house while we were gone, they would have to go out of their way to find things.

We had built a life in that house. And although it was not ours—it was a rental home—it was difficult to think about leaving. It was where we had started our married life together. It was also difficult to narrow down what to take. Having already been told that we would only be allowed one small bag each in case of evacuation, though, we knew our options were limited. Mostly, we stuck to what we had already put in the duffle bag, the essentials. I stared down into the bag I had prepared. I had come to Rwanda with little and I would leave with little. So be it. I packed a change of clothes and made sure that my passport and money were still there where I had put them a few days before. That was basically it. We would have to take only the most essential things and leave the rest stashed behind in hopes they would be there upon our return.

Of course, there was no guarantee that we could return.

While Melanie was busily closing up the house, I headed out to start loading our vehicle. On my way out, I spotted Justin watching me from the doorway of the outer room we had given him when the shooting started. I realized then that I knew very little about him. I knew that he was Hutu, but did this guarantee his safety? Did he have family nearby? Was he afraid for them?

"Come here," I told him, gesturing for him to follow. He removed his hat as he followed me inside. I led him into the kitchen. He spoke to me quietly, as was his nature.

"You are leaving," he observed.

"Yes. We want you to take some food." I began rummaging through the freezer and took out several packages of frozen meat to put into a cooler. "This should last you awhile."

He nodded solemnly, an expression of his gratitude. I closed the freezer door and looked around the room.

"Rice," I said, clapping my hands together and making a beeline for our provisions. I did not even bother to scoop some out for him, opting to hand him whole parcels of it, nearly 50 pounds worth. I helped him lug the food to his room.

"OK," I said, holding out my hand. "Thank you for everything you've done to help us."

He took my right hand, clasping it gently. As is the custom, he placed his left hand over his own right bicep as a sign of respect. It seemed so slow and subdued in the face of my urgency. I was struck with the oddness of it.

"Imana iguma hamwe nawe," he said. *May God be with you.*

"Thank you. And also with you," I told him automatically.

I turned toward the truck. Remembering that I had a large 3' x 4' American flag stashed away in the house, I ran inside to get it. Several minutes later, it was secured to the outside of a homemade topper we had on the back of the red Toyota pick-up truck. Melanie swung her bag in and stepped up into the passenger seat. The small family we were housing climbed into the backseat of the cab behind her. We were ready.

Justin jogged down to the yellow, metal gate and pulled it open for us. We made eye contact as I drove by.

"Thank you," was all I could say. As we pulled onto the streets of Kigali three days into a war zone, I wondered if we would ever see our home again.

"Please, God," I whispered, looking out over the city from our hilltop and glancing back in the mirror at the five lives in the truck with me. Whatever happened now was in God's hands.

INTO THE WATER

1978
GISENYI, RWANDA

Rosa wanted to come with us. Sometimes she did and sometimes she didn't, but this time Tudy leaned her head out the door and called after us as we headed down to the lake. Tudy had on a navy blue print dress and the sides of her hair were pinned back with bobby pins as if she was only half ready to meet the world.

"When are you leaving?" she called, her strong eyes twinkling at us from the doorway.

"Soon, Mom," Judd yelled back, stopping in his track on the grass. Tudy disappeared in the doorway before reappearing moments later.

"Can you wait ten minutes?" she asked. "Rosa wants to come with you into town. And I need her to get some things, too."

"We'll wait. Just tell her to hurry up."

Judd bent down to pick up a stone from out of the grass and flung it far out into the water.

"All right then," said Tudy. "You boys have water with you?"

We held up our canteens and smiled at her. Satisfied, she disappeared back into the house. We headed back down to the lake where a small crowd had gathered around the barge and began the loading process. I nodded to several of the workers who I recognized from around the coffee plantation and tested out my Kinyarwanda on them.

"Mwaramutse," I repeated over and over. *Good morning, good morning.* When they'd ask how I was, I'd answer, "Amakuru yawe."

Judd smiled approvingly at my effort and helped make sure the boat was ready to go. We checked the fuel levels and the fluids.

Fifteen minutes later, we were ready to go—and there was still no Rosa.

"I hope Mom didn't ask her to take care of the toothpicks again," muttered Judd good-naturedly, one eye on his watch.

I laughed. The last time Tudy had asked her to refill the toothpick jar, Rosa had painstakingly cleaned each individual, used toothpick, collected from the previous weeks, not realizing that Tudy kept a supply of fresh ones in the pantry and that she was meant to toss away the old ones.

"She'll be here," I told him, not wanting there to be any friction between mother and son. It was a beautiful day. The sun shone brightly off the slender grasses and sleek banana leaves near the lake's red, muddy edge and birds and bugs whizzed through the air. The place felt alive. *I* felt alive. In all my time on the farm in Minnesota, I had never felt quite so vibrant. There was no feeling in the world that could compare to it.

We made sure everyone was on safely and got everything ready to go. Just as Judd was about to hop off and run back up toward the house, Rosa, wrapped in her usual orange, red and white cloth and head scarf, made an appearance and boarded along with the others.

"Glad to see you," he said to her, to which she just smiled and turned away. I roared the engine into action and we pushed off.

Once a week Judd and I loaded up the barge and headed out across Lake Kivu toward town in order to buy supplies and generally just get out for a change. E.J.'s makeshift barge had grown considerably in popularity since my first visit to Rwanda, and was now a regular passenger carrier. On that particular day, we crammed nearly thirty people onto its deck, the car engine we had mounted and remounted more than a few times since E.J. had originally built the craft, groaning and moaning beneath us. Rosa stood back near the rudder where Judd and I yelled comments back and forth to each other. Every so often, Judd would crouch down and bail water out of the bottom of the boat where the shaft went down to the propeller.

"See what you'd be missing out on if you had decided to stay in Minnesota?" Judd called to me over his shoulder from where he was on bailing duty. He gestured wide over the lake, encompassing the reflecting sun off the water and the surrounding hills and thick trees with a sweep of his arms.

I smiled broadly from where I had a grip on the pole that controlled the rudder. Judd never tired of reminding me how beautiful it was in Rwanda. Not that I could argue, either. As far as I was concerned, there was no place like it in the world. I breathed in and let the scent from the lake penetrate my lungs as deeply as I could. He looked back at me and caught me with eyes closed and chest puffed.

"Now, if only we could find you a wife."

The air in my lungs exploded into half convulsion, half laughter. He and I talked all the time about how great it would be to get married and settle down with somebody, but who to choose from? There wasn't exactly a line-up of eligible American women around, here or back home, dying to become missionary wives in Africa. He rocked self-satisfied on his heels, his arms crossed over his chest and I swerved the rudder ever so slightly, just enough to make him have to grab onto something to stay on his feet. An uncertain yell rose collectively from our passengers and several of them shot me a look. I looked away as if we had only hit a wake or something.

Rosa leaned across and said something to Judd, who laughed and spoke to her in return. When they were finished with their exchange, Judd turned to me.

"She says that if you bump her into the water, she will tell my mother on you."

Rosa shot me a dangerous side-glance and I leaned my head back and laughed.

"Tell her not to worry," I retorted, "If I bump her into the water, I'll come back for her."

"Absolutely," said Judd, very seriously.

"Eventually," I added, bouncing my eyebrows mischievously in Rosa's direction.

"Right, eventually," he was still playing serious with me.

"I mean, as long as she promises not to tell your mother on me, of course."

Judd relayed the deal back to Rosa, whose eyes had now narrowed into slits. She slowly sank to her knees, making as if she were going to scoop a handful of water up and fling it at me.

"Oh no! You do *not* want to do that!" I laughed at her, pointing threateningly at the rudder I held within my power. Several of the people on the barge were by now paying attention to the burgeoning war at the back of the barge and were grinning nervously at us. She made a couple more false motions at me and I continued to shake my head as if to insinuate that I was not the least bit impressed. We were approaching our destination now, and I cut the engine to let the barge glide the rest of the way in relative silence. The waves lapped the sides as everyone waited for the buzz of the engine to wear off and to once again let the stillness of the natural world settle in around and through us.

"3:00," Judd said to everyone in Kinyarwanda. "If you want to catch the barge back, be here no later than 3:00."

He shot a look at Rosa.

"Even you," he teased.

"What? I will not be late," she maintained haughtily in her native tongue. She hung back from the others who had already headed up the bank toward the road and watched us through amused eyes, her arms crossed over her chest.

He rolled his eyes at me.

"She says this every time, that she will not be late."

"And yet," I shrugged. I finished tying up the barge.

"And yet..."

"If you are late," I said to her through Judd, translator by necessity, "We make no promises about the trip home. That is to say, I try my best to hold that rudder steady, but it does sometimes get away from me."

A shocked exclamation escaped from the back of Rosa's throat and she spoke rapidly to Judd.

"She says you had better not or she will scorch your coffee. And anyway, she insists she won't be late."

"We'll see," I said.

Time is not exactly a concern in Rwandan culture. People focus more on events. If something does not get done one day, it's not a big deal. They will just work on it the next day. Similarly, if somebody stops by to say hello while you are in the middle of a project, you had better stop what you are doing and chat with them for a good long while. Nobody has an eye on the clock. Time is not the director of what it is that you are doing; time is what happens while you're doing something else. And for Rosa, it was purely incidental.

"We'll see," repeated Judd.

We walked Rosa up the bank and down the road a ways until we branched off, Judd and me to our errands and Rosa to hers. For all of my teasing, I adored Rosa and I knew she thought I was pretty OK, too. Sure, as a recent college graduate I was sort of goofy at times and not always the best at blending into the culture with my fair white skin, reddish brown hair and glasses, but she had told Judd once that for an *umuzungu*, a white boy, I was all right. Plus, I had found out that she was actually engaged to be married as I had thought, which sort of took the pressure off. We treated her much like a sister without any worries about any romantic misinterpretations or repercussions.

"Let's head over to the café first," suggested Judd. "Then we can go get supplies for my dad."

"Sounds good," I agreed. Part of the reason we had come over that day was because E.J. needed some new parts for the hydroelectric plant. He had been working his fingers to the bone with that project. Tudy was constantly reminding him to take a break and trying to entice him to stop for a while with passionfruit—*maracuja*—juice, and sweet cakes, but he was relentless. As far as he was concerned, the Bible school needed electricity and by golly, it was going to get it. It was largely the reason I had come back over, after all. That hydroelectric plant not only had the power to pull E.J. out of bed every morning before the crack of dawn, but it had also pulled me halfway around the world. If it weren't for E.J.'s dream, I might not have ever gotten the letter suggesting I come back. Dreams, well-conceived, seem to be contagious that way.

We headed out for our stops, filling up on local fare, and making our usual rounds in town. By the time 3:00 rolled around, we were hot, exhausted from the day, loaded down by our burdens, and ready to head back. There was only one problem. Rosa had not come back to the barge.

"I'm going to throw her into the lake," I told Judd with a grin, looking around at the people who had dutifully made it back on time.

"I tell you what," he said, "You can throw *me* into the lake if you want. It's hot and I'm cooked."

"Well, I'm throwing someone in the lake today," I responded. "And I won't be far behind."

We waited ten minutes, twenty...thirty! Finally, at nearly forty minutes past three, we saw Rosa's bright floral headscarf bobbing through the line of people. She was walking, not running—and not the slightest bit concerned that nearly thirty people were waiting on her. We watched her through heavy lids as she strolled down the bank with her bags and stepped gingerly onto the barge. She nodded once at us—more a challenge than a greeting—and then took her place across from us on the opposite side. I bit my lip to keep from laughing and started up the engine.

We retraced our route through the water back to the plantation. People were tired from the day's outing and talked little over the drone of the engine. Finally, after an hour or so, we made it back. Just as I cut the engine, Rosa turned and looked at us. It was only a brief look, but it said much. In a nutshell, it said, "I say what is late, and not you."

"Oh, no she did not," I muttered to Judd, who had begun laughing immediately upon "the look."

"I think she did," he said, his shoulders bouncing.

Come here, I gestured with my hands. Rosa turned away as if she had not seen me.

"Rosa!" I called out from my place at the rudder. I eased the barge up to the loading point. A few of the passengers hopped off and began tying up the barge to the dock. We were still in reasonably deep water.

Not wanting to cause a scene in front of the others, she turned to look at me. The language of her eyes had not changed much since her first look. I gestured for her to come to the back of the boat again. Without much of a choice, she steadied her way across the small deck until she was next to us.

"You were late," I told her with a false sternness. Judd translated for me and she shrugged.

"I believe I made you a promise," I said.

She wrinkled up her forehead at me as if I were crazy.

"I know you know what I'm talking about," I told her. "And I'm afraid it's time to pay your dues."

I leaned down as she had done earlier and splashed a little water at her. She shrieked and splashed some back at me, laughing. I grabbed a big handful and flung it at her this time.

"That's it!" I yelled, amidst her giggles. "You're going over!" And with that, I grabbed her around the waist and flung her into the lake. She shrieked as she hit the water, thrashing and kicking wildly. Realizing in a flash that she didn't know how to swim, I dove in after her, nearly clonking heads with Judd who had had the same realization as I did. He grabbed one arm, I grabbed the other, and somehow the three of us made it back to the shore amidst the tirade coming from Rosa and the laughing cheers from our recent passengers.

Somewhere in the background I heard Tudy asking what all the fuss was. I looked up at her looking down on us, fists on hips, shaking her head like she was about to reprimand the three of us. Rosa wrung out the water in her skirt, stopping suddenly to catch her breath, bent forward at the waist with her hands on her knees. All of a sudden, Rosa's shoulders began to bounce.

Oh no, I thought, *we made her cry*. Judd and I looked at each other, biting our lips and realizing that we had inadvertently crossed the line with our teasing. We hung our heads, bracing for the lecture that was rightfully due us, when we began to hear a noise—a high pitch wheezing sound. It was Rosa. She was laughing.

Judd and I glanced nervously between each other and Tudy. By now Rosa was upright, holding her stomach and laughing so hard she could barely talk. After a minute or so, she finally managed a sentence to Judd.

"She's never been in the lake before," he grinned.

Tudy looked back and forth between us and I just knew then that she was about to let us have it.

"Well, I'd say it was high time, then!" she snorted.

Judd and I looked at Tudy and her unexpected assessment and it was all over. Before we knew it, we were all four of us shaking with laughter amidst the small crowd that had gathered around us. Somewhere in the midst of it, Judd slipped away from us, grabbed a bucketful of water and unloaded it on his mother, who shrieked even louder than Rosa had and dove for a bucket of her own. Soon, we were chasing each other all around the compound with buckets of water and laughing at the top of our voices until it was time to clean up and start preparations for dinner. And, I suppose it goes without saying, I avoided the coffee the next morning!

ON THE MOVE

APRIL 9, 1994
KIGALI, RWANDA

We had not gone far, a half of a block, when we saw that what had been happening around us was far worse than our imaginations had allowed us to realize. The homes of some of our neighbors were in shambles, their contents blown to bits and spread across their yards. Roofs had holes in them, doors were missing, and windows were in pieces in the street, while other houses were charred shells. From our position on the road, we could see that across the city, smoke plumes rose in the damp weather, making them appear as low lying, darkened clouds.

Several houses down, a door opened as we passed and a small child emerged, waving. Reflexively, Melanie raised a hand and smiled at the boy. Close to eight-years old, he was one of the children that came regularly to Melanie's Wednesday afternoon kids' club at our house. I remembered more than once walking in on him sitting at our kitchen table, fist clenched around a fat Crayola or watching him run with the neighborhood kids as they played Red Rover or Freeze Tag. She seemed to catch herself then and stilled her fingers as a sadness spread through her.

"What's going to happen to him?" She asked, more to her window than to me. A tear escaped from the corner of her eyes and she caught it mid-cheek.

We understood that the boy and his family were most certainly Hutu or they would not have been left alive at all. Even so, who could predict what would happen in the following days? They were in a war zone, a civil war, brother against brother and nobody was taking prisoners. I reached out and placed a hand on her knee. There was no answer I could give her.

We were approaching a small market and I could see that there were only soldiers and militia members out on the streets. No one was selling anything that day and the stalls stood empty save for a few rotting vegetables stuck in the corners.

A man ahead of us on the side of the road turned to look at us as we passed. He was dressed in a brown T-shirt and blue jeans and wore flip-flops on his feet. He noticed the flag on the side of our vehicle before glancing at me behind the wheel, then quickly turned back to the road before him and kept walking. It was only fleeting, but there was something off about his eyes. It was if he was not in his right mind somehow, like he was half-crazed. I saw then that he had a long piece of wood in his right hand. It was stained with blood.

A shock wave went through my body and my senses prickled with awareness. It was then that I noticed a large pile of something on the road next to the end of the stalls. Was it wood? But why was there a large stack of wood on the street? I stared at it for a couple of seconds as my brain refused to make sense out of what I was seeing. When it hit me what it was, I looked away as quickly as I could before the image imprinted itself permanently in my dreams, bodies, five or six of them. I quickly closed my eyes and squeezed them shut tight, but it was too late for my memory. How could I ever forget?

"Close your eyes," I told Melanie. When she didn't answer, I looked over at her. Her eyes were already closed.

"I don't want to have nightmares," she said quietly. "You'll have to tell me when to close them. Please," she begged.

We passed the market and the bodies, my foot firmly on the accelerator. Behind me, I vaguely noticed that the kids had crouched down beneath the window line. While my mind struggled to understand the world around us, there was one thing I understood perfectly. We had to get out of there. I had to get Melanie out of there.

Taking the route that the soldiers had described past the low-lying marsh on the left and the military camp on the right, we were able to get into the main part of the city. All along the way, we passed numerous roadblocks, many marked by yet another pile of the fallen. All were manned by young men bearing *mpanga*—machetes—or clubs in their hands. Every time we approached, I spoke as quickly as I could.

"Close your eyes."

Before I could finish the brief sentence, her hands flew to her face, her fingers pressed to her eyelids. She spoke scarcely a word the entire trip, only commenting once or twice about how she hoped our friends had been granted such easy passage as we had. With the topper on the back of our truck, it seemed only logical that we would be stopped and searched. And yet, each checkpoint we arrived at would be yawning wide open for us to pass through, the flag of our country seemingly acting as our passport.

"It's like the parting of the Red Sea," commented Melanie, somewhat incredulously.

We held our breath in the cab, praying that we would be allowed to pass. Each time, nobody made any attempt to stop us. It was as if we were being accompanied by angels, unseen.

We took a back road uphill toward the center of Kigali where the US Embassy was. As we neared the top, we spotted several large army trucks sitting crossways in the road where we needed to turn left at a stop sign. Having no choice, we stopped and waited to let a semi carrying a backhoe coming from the right turn in front of us. Following the semi was a large orange tandem axle dump truck. I thought nothing of it until I suddenly realized that dangling off the top was a mesh of legs and arms. The truck was literally overflowing with bodies. I realized then the purpose of the backhoe. "Close them, now!" It was all I could choke out.

The driver looked at us as we waited, closely examining the passengers in our truck. Behind me in the back seat, the woman began to whisper rapidly. From the three children on the floor, there was not a sound.

With the large trucks blocking our left turn, we abandoned our route to the Embassy and drove straight across the intersection. There was a hotel there, large and elegant and surrounded by large trees and blooming bushes. I drove the truck into the half-empty lot, parked and got out, locking the doors behind us. We headed toward the hotel doors, the woman holding onto her children and rushing them forward. There was no time to lose.

We walked toward the glass doors of the Hôtel des Milles Collines—known now through much of the world as "Hotel Rwanda"—one foot in front of the other.

For all we had seen, it hardly seemed possible we were walking at all. We should have been beyond function, incapacitated. People were dying in their homes and in the damp, dirty streets at the hand of men walking around with clubs and *mpanga*. What we had seen was unconscionable. It defied human civility at any level. It was as if the entire country had succumbed to a madness that was bestial, demonic, even.

And yet, there we were, walking into a world class four star hotel lobby filled with business people, tourists and government representatives. There were plush couches and wall-to-wall elegant carpeting. Uniformed staff visibly worked the desk and anticipated needs. People sat around in the lounge areas and conversed in groups. While there was a definite tension in the air, it was an odd scene to step into after what we had come through. Had I been thinking clearly, I would have marveled at the seeming normality of it. As it was, I could only wonder at the fact that I was functioning at all and not melting down. It was as if I were seeing the world around me through protective glass.

What's wrong with me? I wondered. *Why can't I feel?*

Melanie, it seemed, was not acting any different than I was. Together, we were numb from our emotions as if a heavy door separated them from our thoughts. Our actions and decisions were based on what needed to be done rather than our fears. Psychologists describe this phenomenon as a byproduct of shock. I can tell you firsthand that it is one of God's greatest gifts.

I watched my wife as she stopped in her tracks a little inside the doorway, her tall frame upright and alert. She wore a simple dress and her short brown hair fell somewhat relaxed over her ears. Her eyes through the round frames of her glasses were sharp and keen. With her bag slung over her shoulder, she scanned the many faces around us.

"I don't see them," she said once I had backtracked to her side.

I joined her in looking around, knowing without explanation for whom she was searching. She was looking for Laurie and Gary Scheer, Phil and Mimi Bjorklund, and Scott and Cindy Mueller, among others. She was looking for the other missionaries in our group.

A familiar face appeared then in front of us. It was the woman we had brought with us. Her children stood huddled at her side.

"I would like to stay here," she informed us.

"I think that's probably a good choice," answered Melanie gently. She reached out and touched the top of the youngest child's head. He pulled back close to his mother.

"Thank you," she said. "Thank you for risking your own safety to help us." Turning to the lounge, she led her children to a cluster of chairs and they sat together, their shoulders and legs touching.

We walked slowly through the lobby, acclimating ourselves to the new surroundings. There were many other westerners there, as well as people from around the world, but none we recognized. I approached a man in his thirties or forties standing next to a counter. By his dress style in combination with a large camera he had strapped crossways to his chest, I guessed he was an American or Canadian. At any rate, I knew he didn't live there. I had met or seen every Westerner who lived in the entire country at one time or another. There just weren't that many of us.

"So, what's the word?" I asked him. "Are they talking about evacuation?"

An interesting thing about being in the midst of a crisis: the need to soften a potential conversationalist into providing information is moot. There is no small talk required. Information is requested and granted freely.

"Word is the American Embassy is getting a road convoy together," he told me. His accent placed his origins somewhere in the southern US.

"Is there someone to talk to here?" I asked him, "A US Embassy representative or possibly from the UN?"

"Second floor, Room 217," he told me. "Door's wide open."

He was staring off in such a way that I could sense he had more to say. I waited.

"Can't believe this is happening," he said distantly. "They said it was a risk, but nobody saw this coming. Not *this*."

I had no way of knowing what his story was, but I nodded all the same. Here I had been living in the country on and off since 1975, and I would never have imagined that it would have spiraled into such violence. I thought back to before 1990. I had never so much as heard a single gunshot. I remember being surprised to learn that anybody within the country even had a bullet in their possession. Add to that the fact that Rwanda claimed to be 80% Christian. These people are supposed to love and worship the same God I do. These people have heard about grace and love and forgiveness. They know of the sacrifice His Son made for all of us. How this could have happened was beyond me. It was beyond any of us. It remains so even today.

Even in the midst of it, I had to stay focused on what was happening outside. If I let my mind drift for even a moment, I found myself snapped back into the jarring reality of the situation with a renewed jolt. My mind rebelled against it—fought the very idea of it—so that the minute I let my guard down it pushed the reality of it right out of my head like it was dropping the weight of it out of a window. As soon as I blinked and saw it there, lying on the ground before me, I was struck with the heaviness of it all over again. It had not actually gone anywhere. It was down there, no right here, waiting to be pushed out again and again and again. Is it any wonder that people who go through the unfathomable, cease finally to feel?

I wanted to reach out to the man beside me. In the end, I could not. I cannot explain this other than to say once again that my emotions were in a cycle of shutting down. Emotions, in a situation of life or death, are a luxury that leaves a person vulnerable. After the initial confrontation of witnessing any horrible act or scene, they are the first thing to go. This man was safe where he was, leaning against a countertop with his camera strapped to him. I needed to move on. There were others I was not sure about. I would concern myself with them. This was not a conscious decision. It is yet another function of one of the phases of shock: do what needs to be done. I have heard stories of people who have moved automobiles off of people while in the midst of shock, as if overcome with some kind of superhuman power. Those people moved automobiles; I placed one foot in front of the other. Forward motion was my "automobile".

Melanie and I excused ourselves and headed upstairs to find Room 217. The air inside the hotel was laced with many languages, Swahili, French, English, Kinyrwandan, and virtually vibrated with energy. The second floor, however, was much quieter and more subdued. Not far down the hall we spotted a cluster of people speaking together. We headed toward them and peered into the room to find a man speaking into a two-way radio.

"Are you the one organizing a convoy?" I asked. He held up a hand as a male voice on the other end of the radio crackled into the room. He wore dark slacks and a button down shirt.

"Are you American citizens?" He asked us, snatching a clipboard off the edge of the table he sat behind.

"Yes," we told him.

"You are going to want to go over to the American Club. We're preparing a road convoy to take our folks out of here."

"How soon?" I asked.

"As soon as we can," he answered. "If you head over now, you won't miss them."

Melanie looked over at me wide-eyed. We seemed to be thinking the same thing.

"We can't leave without them, Gary. We just can't. They're our family."

"I know," I said to her. "Thanks," I told the man.

We made our way back down the stairs and through the crowded lobby. Glancing at the counter, I saw that the man I had spoken to earlier was gone. We pushed our way through the clusters of people until we made it back outside into the diffuse light.

"Maybe they are already at the American Club," Melanie suggested as we walked across the parking lot toward our truck. I took her hand.

"Maybe they are."

THE JESUS FILM

1986
SOUTHWESTERN RWANDA

I bumped and jostled my way down the long dirt road in my new maroon double cab Toyota Hilux, purchased for me by the mission organization and now mine to use on this, my third trip back. In the back were a generator, a projector, a screen, a tent, some food, water and basic necessities and a map. I eyed this latter every so often. I was in unfamiliar territory, having driven the length of the country to the southwestern side of Rwanda.

I was not technically supposed to have begun my mission work yet. I was a full-timer now, having chosen finally to make a life of missions in Rwanda. I loved Rwanda—both the people and the place—and it just felt right to continue on the path on which I had started. Thus, I had gone back to Minnesota to finish up my studies at Northwestern and made preparations through World Venture to return to Rwanda as a full-time missionary. In December of 1985, I said good-bye to my family once again, boarded a plane, and headed back over the waters to the heart of Africa, not to return for four more years.

It was a dramatic departure at the airport this time, with everybody in the family sniffing their good-byes. Christmas was only a couple of weeks away, and it was on everyone's mind that I would not be there to share it with them. With a heavy heart, I ruminated over the decision the entire first leg of the journey until we landed in New York. I was sad, but I was also excited. I could feel it escalating within me with each passing mile. By the time I was ready to continue the next leg of the journey on the next plane, my head was clear and my heart was on fire. It was what I was meant to do; I felt it in my bones.

I knew it would be different this time. To begin with, I was on my own. Judd was not meeting me as he was involved in another project for the time being. That alone was going to be quite a change. But there was another absence that I knew would hit me even harder once I was there and felt the emptiness where he once was.

I had not been back long from my second trip over before I heard about the accident. It was E.J. He had been working on his obsession, the hydroelectric plant that provided power for the Bible school and for the coffee plant. He wanted to make some repairs to the jetty, built to provide shelter from the waves for the boats there. He had in his hand a rotary hammer. He was familiar with this tool, having used it many times before to drill holes for blasting. He would drill the hole, put in a stick of dynamite, light the fuse and then stand back and wait. If it didn't go off, he would walk up to the dynamite, pull the fuse, replace it with a new one, and light it again. This day, however, he was not using dynamite. He simply wanted to drill some holes into a stone wall. On its own, it should not have been a dangerous project at all—except for the fact that he was standing with an electric power tool in an inch or so of water. When he plugged in the tool, he discovered too late that the rotary hammer had a short in it. He was killed instantly. It would seem that Tudy was right all along—the water would be respected.

As I was home at the time, there was little that I could do in the way of offering help to Tudy or Judd. I had heard that Judd's siblings were there, so I took some comfort from that. It would be strange going back to Rwanda without E.J. there. His had been such a large presence, despite his gentle manner. Nobody could question it: E.J. had left far too soon. There was still so much that needed to be done.

So much so that now that I was back in Rwanda full-term, I could hardly stand to wait around for my official mission work to begin. I was chomping at the bit. Even so, I was not exactly able to pick up where I had left off before. It may have been my third time back, but the rule was clear: the first year of a new full-term missionary was to be spent in language immersion. Active missions work was not to begin until Year Two.

Language immersion. For me this was not exactly a simple task. I had grown up needing no more than the English I had been raised with in small town Minnesota. McDonald's French Fries were just about the most foreign thing I ever encountered in my youth. And now, I was expected to meet regularly with a language tutor daily, after which I would be sent on my own—sink or swim—into town where I would practice what I had learned. Even so, I did my best and tried to practice patience, mostly.

Checking the map once again, I turned off of the main dirt road and veered west. Glancing at my watch, I could see that I would still have plenty of time to set up, even though I had been held up by an accident on the main tar road back in Kigali. Even so, I was ready to get out of that dusty truck and get set up. On the seat beside me was a box, in which I could see the reel of film peeking out at me. I was not really breaking the rules, I thought with a smile. I was not talking to anyone or working directly with people at the vocational or Bible school. It was more like a side job, a hobby. And anyway, I was supposed to be venturing out on my own to practice my Kinyarwanda. They wanted my first year to be focused on language immersion. What better way was there than to hit the road and end up in a village where I had never been before? I was just stepping things up a notch. A little bit of extra credit.

By the time I arrived, I was hot and my joints were aching from the jostling the road had given me. Checking my directions, I made my way through the narrow dirt streets until I found the church. The pastor, a tall, narrow faced man with gentle eyes met me at the door with a handshake. I remembered him from before, when he had done his training at the Bible School in Gisenyi during my second visit to Rwanda. He had been kind to me then and I was happy to see that he had managed to establish a church in his village. Back in the 1970s, our organization had forty churches in all of Rwanda. At the time, it had been their goal to double that number. "80 churches by '80" was the slogan. But by 1980, we had far surpassed that. And by 1985, the year I started as a full-term missionary, we had already tripled the number. We were not the only denomination involved in aggressive evangelism at the time, but we were certainly at the forefront. Other denominations that were over there, too, were the Free Methodists and the Anglicans, or Episcopals.

"Wariye?" He asked me. *Have you eaten?*

"Ntabwo shonge," I told him, assuring him that I was not the least bit hungry yet, and asked if it would be all right if I began setting up. I was anxious to make sure everything was ready to go.

He climbed into the cab of the Toyota with me and pointed me down the road. The soccer, or football field, as they would have referred to it, was a large, flat area surrounded by overgrown native grasses around the edges and lined with vine-draped trees. It was late afternoon, and the sun hit the smooth banana leaves that rose like feathers in a cap above the others with a shining brilliance. I drove over the red earth toward one end and began setting up the screen, driving stakes into the ground in order to keep it steady. Already, curious passersby stopped to watch what was happening, and occasionally made their way over to ask questions. There was not a soul in the entire village that had not already heard that there would be a film that night. Word of mouth travels quickly in those towns, and with films as scarce as they were, this was considered big news.

Based on previous experience, I knew that it would be a big turnout and that we could have a thousand or more people gathering to watch. Tonight would be no different. Most of the people in that area had never seen a movie before in their lives. People would come.

It had only been a few years since our organization had translated the well-known three-hour movie called simply The Jesus Film about the life, death and resurrection of Jesus into Kinyarwanda. It had been well received, too. Even though I had only been at it for less than a year, venturing out to show it two or three times only on weekends, I figure I showed it to nearly 100,000 people that first year.

As we worked, the pastor asked me about Gisenyi and the progress we had made on various projects. He wanted to know about the number of students at the Bible College, as well as in the vocational school. When he asked about E.J., I stopped what I was doing.

"We miss him," I told him, overcome suddenly by a feeling of reverence. I had visited the hill overlooking Cymbili where he was buried just that week. I thought about Tudy, whom I had left behind earlier that afternoon after having helped her fix one of the hinges on her front door. I had been trying to help take care of her. My friends, the Bjorklunds, had also been keeping a watchful eye over her there. We all had.

"He kept that place running."

"He was a good man," he agreed. "He believed in what he was doing. If it were not for him, I would not be here." He swept his hands wide as if to encompass the entire village, his church, and even what we were doing that very moment. We were finished setting up the screen now and he looked me in the eyes and placed a hand on my shoulder. "Now you will let me show you some hospitality," he said. "My wife has been cooking all day for you and will never forgive me if I do not bring you home with me for a bite of supper before the film. I promise I will not keep you late."

We had an hour and a half before the sun would go down, so I happily agreed. He took me to his home, a round, mud plastered hut with a thatched roof, where his wife and five children waited for us with steaming plates of manioc dumplings and a stew made of *isombe*—the dried manioc leaves—and red beans. We ate with windows and doors closed, as is Rwandan culture—so as to not let anyone else know how much or how little we had to eat. The atmosphere inside the little home, although warm, was congenial and light and the children were delightful and full of bright smiles.

True to his word, he made sure we were back out the door as quickly as possible. I thanked his wife for the meal and we left together in the truck and headed for the outer edge of the village. I had mounted a loudspeaker to my truck and handed him the microphone.

"Please?" I asked him.

He looked at it suspiciously for a few moments, before testing it. Outside the truck, his voice boomed through the airwaves. He smiled broadly at me, a glint in his eye, and then got to work, chuckling to himself all the while.

"Come to the football field at sundown for a film! It's the chance of a lifetime! You won't want to miss! Don't be late! Come watch a film!" *Au cinema! Au Cinema! nziza chani!* (A film, a film, it is the best!)

By the time we arrived at the field, a small crowd of men, women and children had begun to gather. We positioned the truck so that we could run the projector off the generator out of the back. It was a beautiful evening with no clouds in sight, so I did not feel the necessity to set up the tent over the equipment should it rain. Everything was running smoothly. Really, it could not have been a more perfect night.

As we set up, people continued to come. At first, I was thinking that the turnout looked like what I was used to—and then I began to look around. People kept coming. There were easily 2,000 people now, standing around in the half-light. As the sun sank low behind the banana trees, I kept looking out toward the street, but the crowd showed no signs of slowing down. Mothers, dressed in brightly colored wraps with children strapped to their backs and *igitenge*, or head wraps, on their heads stood together in groups with their older children running merrily around together. Men dressed in pants and shirts stood barefoot in clusters, both on the field and on the fringes. As the sky grew darker and darker, small groups of men drunk on banana beer would show up, laughing loudly and yelling comments back and forth above the crowd, people of all walks of life, farmer, cattle herder, and merchant, gathered together in good cheer. There was no division among them, Hutu and Tutsi, alike—many crossing borders within the same family. I remember thinking on it even then. I knew from hearing the stories that there had been violent problems between them in the 1950s. I had heard rumors of uprisings and killings. And yet, any tension that had been between them from the civil unrest 30 years prior was nowhere to be seen that day in 1985. Hutu men laughed with Tutsi men just the same as if they were brothers. And many of them were.

As I turned on the projector that night, with now nearly 3,000 faces glowing in the light from the screen, I thanked God for grace and for the healing that could bring back together a nation that had been torn apart so relatively recently. If God could restore peace in such a situation as that, then He could do it anywhere.

"This is some film," the pastor told me at one point. We had seen the birth of the Christ child, the overturning of the tables in the temple as a boy, the choosing of the disciples. The soldiers had just pressed the crown of thorns into his head when I decided to go check on one of the lines holding up the screen. A breeze had come up during the film and I was concerned that it might topple if it was not held securely enough. I had seen it so many times by now that I knew it by heart, even in Kinyarwanda. I nodded back at him in agreement, and strolled up through the crowd, gently

THE JESUS FILM

pushing my way through as I went. In Rwanda, people stand for everything and a movie is no different. Men, women and children kept on their feet throughout the entirety of the film.

As I walked, I could hear the people talking about the film. With no established movie culture yet, people would commonly talk out loud throughout the entire show. On the one hand, it can be very disruptive. On the other hand, I had access to instant feedback. As they pushed and kicked Jesus around and forced him to carry his own cross up the long road to Golgotha, people in the crowd around me cried out at the injustice of it and in sympathy of the pain. Seeing what our Lord had done for all of us was an overwhelming experience for many of them—made all the more poignant by their misconception that they were seeing the actual crucifixion of Christ. Since the vast majority of them had never seen a movie before, they had no real concept of actors. As I walked through the crowd, I could hear the comments they would make that confirmed this. At the front, I made some adjustments to one of the stakes and toggled the others for good measure. When I made my way back to the truck, I leaned in to the pastor.

"You will need to perhaps explain that these are actors, but that the story is real," I suggested gently.

He nodded.

"Yes. I will do just that."

Typically, at the end of the film, the pastor of the area would stand up in front of everyone and say a few words, inviting people to make a decision to follow Jesus. Most of the pastors took this opportunity to explain that the film was made by modern day actors and not a documentary filmed on location nearly 2000 years ago. It never mattered. People would raise their hands in droves, and pray the prayer of repentance and forgiveness with him. It was—and still is—a powerful film.

On screen, the soldiers drove stakes into Jesus' hands. From all over the field, there were cries from men and women, alike. Even the men who had come in drunk on banana beer at the beginning were riveted to the screen. It was a tense moment, and highly emotional. And that's right about the time when it happened. The film broke.

"Hey!" People called out. "Where did it go?"

"Sorry!" I yelled back in Kinyarwanda. I leapt to my feet and hovered over the projector, trying to assess what had happened. I needed a flashlight. I began frantically looking around.

"We came to watch a film!" yelled a male voice from the darkness. There was no moon that night and the field had been shrouded in an inky black.

"Yeah, that's right. We're here to watch a film and we're not leaving until we do!"

"What happened to Jesus?" yelled another. "I want to know what happened!"

I jumped off the bed of the truck and reached into the cab to switch on the headlights. Several people nearby called out, startled.

"Please, everyone. Be patient. We are trying to repair it." It was the pastor's voice over the loudspeaker. He had reached in through the passenger side of the window and grabbed the mike. Our eyes met across the cab and he winked at me.

Thank goodness.

I found the flashlight in the cab and raced back around to the back of the truck where the projector was, tripping on my own shoe as I did it.

"Whoa," I said, under my breath. The last thing I needed was to add an injury to the situation. It was tense enough as it was. I climbed back up into the back of the truck and started to work on the film. One of the reels was stuck. I couldn't get it to move.

Focused on the beam of the flashlight, I could hear the noise escalating around me. People were not happy. There were calls back and forth demanding that I start the movie back up. Some of the rowdier men were beginning to sound threatening. My mind flashed back to a time earlier that year when Phil Bjorklund and I had gotten caught in a mob outside of our duplex on the mission compound. It was students at the vocational school that time, purportedly unhappy with the food rations they were getting. We never did understand what it was really about—we'd been eating off the same rations they had been when we were at the school, and thought they were just fine. Furthermore, we had nothing to do with the rations. We did not say how much a person could eat at mealtime—that was from the administration at the school. Even so, a group of about thirty young men had cut our electric power and gathered with bed sheets over their heads around our compound, thinking Phil and I could do something about it. It was a bunch of yelling at first, but finally descended into rock and brick throwing. As they lobbed rocks at us over the three-foot. compound wall in the night, Phil and I ducked behind for safety, yelling back at them as we stood our ground. We had nothing to give them. We had no power whatsoever. They finally backed off when somebody shattered our kerosene lamp and they realized they weren't getting anywhere. Most of them were expelled the next day.

Fearing the situation could develop into a similar situation—only now with 3,000 people instead of thirty—I bumbled through fixing the projector as quickly as I could. In the background, the drunk men yelled insults and threats while the crowd bucked and swayed with impatience. Finally—*finally*—I got the reel to move again. I patched up the film and set it to work. A cheer rippled through the audience and I sat down with a thud.

The audience watched with rapt attention through the rest of the film as Jesus died and then returned from the grave to talk to them. By the time the pastor got up in front to talk to everyone, there were many in the audience who were openly weeping. He invited anyone who wanted to accept the gift of grace to raise their hands and to step forward. Many were saved that night. Considering the circumstances, I count myself among them.

REFUSING TO GO

APRIL 9, 1994
KIGALI, RWANDA

The life of a missionary is not unlike the life of a member of the Armed Forces. There is a camaraderie among those of us in the field. We have spent significant amounts of time developing relationships. We have laughed together, trained together, sacrificed together, cried together, and prayed together. We have clung together when confronted with culture shock. We have celebrated together over the success of a project. We have watched each other's children grow up and the children have called us "aunt" or "uncle." We have watched each other grow, personally and spiritually. We join together to win people back to Him by using the example He gave us to love and care for the needs of one another, thus pushing back evil in the world. Like the Armed Forces, we are fighting a battle, although unseen. And, also like the Armed Forces, no one gets left behind.

The fact that we had not yet heard news of our colleagues was troubling to us. Having been told that people were being routed to the American Club, only a block or so away from the Hôtel des Mille Collines, Melanie and I wasted no time in making our way there. We had seen enough on the streets on our way over to understand that there was risk associated with any amount of travel, regardless of how brief the trip. We got in the truck, fastened our seatbelts, and made a bolt for it.

Luckily, the streets were deserted. It may not have been a long trip, but both of us breathed a sigh of relief when we arrived in the parking lot of the American Club only a few minutes later.

"Thank you, Lord," I said, pulling out the keys and locking the doors behind us. We took nothing for granted at that point.

Inside the American Club, we were immediately directed to Laura Lane, an official I had dealt with before. Tall and thin with dark blond hair that fell to her shoulders, an elegant straight nose and keen blue eyes, Laura was the consular officer at the US Embassy. Her job was to act as liaison between the US Ambassador, the Tutsi rebel army and the Hutu-led government army. She recognized us right away.

"The Bennetts are here," she said, checking something off on a piece of paper. Only the flicker of a smile crossed her face. She was all business. Waving a 2-way radio at us, she added, "They told me you were on your way."

Normally the American Club was filled with a more festive atmosphere with music playing and people walking casually together, chatting about business or travel. Today was markedly different with people standing in clusters and speaking in hushed tones about what they had seen on their way over. Many were visibly in a stage of shock. It felt more like the lobby of an ER than a social club.

"Have you heard from any of these people?" She asked, holding out the list of Americans in the city to us. There were 258 names on the list.

We took several moments to scan the names, pausing at the names of our friends only to discover that they had not checked in yet. We told her we had not seen any of them.

Laura shook her head, clearly agitated.

"Someone needs to go out and try and get other Americans who are stranded in their homes," she said. "We need troops."

"Aren't they sending any?" I asked.

"Who?" she asked. "The US? The UN? Your guess is as good as mine," she said. "They've gotten an earful from me, I'll tell you that much."

As we were speaking, another missionary couple we recognized pushed through the doors. They were Southern Baptists with a different organization.

"Oh, thank you, Lord," said Melanie, rushing toward them. We met somewhere in between and there was a flurry of information exchanged between us. Verne and Sandy Sivage had not seen the extent we had, but had seen enough. Melanie and I hugged each of their necks tight and ran down the list of our mutual friends and colleagues. They had no more information than we did.

"Excuse me," came a voice behind us. It was Laura again. "We are preparing a road convoy in the next couple of hours," she told us. "Stay in this area so that we can communicate. We'll let you know when it's time to leave."

"We're not interested in joining this convoy until we hear from our colleagues. I'm sorry, but we have to know they are safe," I said, shaking my head. The Sivages nodded solemnly in agreement.

Laura looked at us like we were out of our heads.

"I don't know if you've noticed, but things are bad out there. You need to go while you can."

I shook my head slowly at her and attempted a smile.

"I know you're doing your job, Laura, but we have a responsibility to our people. They are not just our colleagues, but our friends. Our family," I added, glancing at Melanie. "We're not leaving until we know they are safe."

She looked down at the list.

"Just who are we talking about here?"

I pointed out the names on the list from our group. The Scheers. The Bjorklunds. The Muellers.

"Mr. and Mrs. Bennett. It is entirely possible that they have found another safe way out." She looked back and forth at us, pleadingly. "You need to go with the convoy. It's not safe here."

All we could do was to shrug back at her. We were not going to budge.

We could see that she understood, but her duty was to get us on that convoy. Visibly frustrated, she walked off to the table where she had been stationed before we walked in. There is no question she was actively and commendably coordinating the evacuation of a large number of US citizens in the middle of a violent crisis. People were not supposed to *not* want to be evacuated. We were officially being difficult. I cleared my throat.

"OK," I said to Melanie. "We need to figure out what is being done to find our people." We began scanning the room for someone else who looked remotely official. Aside from the average businessperson, resident or unlucky tourist, however, it appeared we were out of luck. I looked over at the television at the side of the room, noticing that it was off with the power outage. We needed information. Remembering a few UN soldiers outside the door, I excused myself from Melanie and the others.

"May I ask you a question," I said when I was finally able to get the attention of a rather large man dressed in a khaki uniform.

He nodded curtly.

"Are you actively going out after people? I mean citizens of other countries."

"We're doing what we can, sir," he told me, looking past me over my head.

"But some of my colleagues are out there still," I told him. "Without communications, how are they going to know to come here?"

"I don't know about that, sir. Like I said, we're doing everything we can."

I put my hands on my hips and stared a hole deep into the ground. I could feel my temper rising and I wanted to make sure I did not add to the problems already swirling around us. I understood Laura's frustration we had sensed inside. Why were the only visible UN officers posted at doorways? Why wasn't anyone from the world community stepping in to help stop the killing? Where was the leadership throughout all of this? Why was the US silent? Was the official stance that they were just going to sit back and let it happen? What was happening around us was beyond civil war, this was a blatant genocide.

Genocide.

The word washed over me like a wave as footage from World War II played on my mind. When the world found out about what the Nazis were doing to the Jews, they stepped in to help. Where was our help? Was it because Rwanda was not part of the "first world"? Was it because we were in Africa?

I exhaled once, slowly, and looked back up at the officer.

"Are troops being sent?"

The officer continued to stare past me.

"I know. You're doing what you can," I answered for him.

I could see that I was not getting anywhere, so I went back inside. Our colleagues were still out there somewhere in the midst of a volatile situation and nobody was stepping in to help. More than anything, I wanted to get in my truck and drive to their houses to see if they were safe. How else would we know? The streets were no place to be, though. There was no disputing that. I could not put Melanie in that kind of danger. And if I went alone, I risked leaving her a widow.

Whatever happens, Melanie had said on the way over from the hotel, *we stay together.*

But we needed to know that they were safe. We could not—*would not*—go anywhere without them. I didn't know what to do. My hands were tied.

Please, Lord, show us a way to our friends, I prayed silently.

"What did they say?" asked Melanie. "Are they collecting people to bring them here?"

I held out my open hands. Her guess was as good as mine.

After a while, a tense Laura Lane approached Melanie and me sitting in a couple of chairs. She looked at the two of us and softened.

"If you're not going to go on this convoy, will you do one thing for me?"

"Sure," we shrugged. "We want to help."

"Just go down to the bar and give people whatever they ask for."

Melanie and I looked at each other. Somewhere in the background, a needle scratched across a record.

"The bar?" I repeated, but she was already walking away and expecting us to follow.

"Gary?" asked Melanie, matching me stride for stride. She had the kind of look on her face that wives reserve for their husbands when they are trying to communicate a secret message. In her case, the message was, "Gary, Darling. Neither you nor I have ever drunk a drop of alcohol in our entire lives. Please rethink what you are about to commit us to before it's too late."

I met her encoded message with a raise of the eyebrows and a shrug. In my case, the message was, "When in Rome?"

Having been raised Conservative Baptist, we had not been raised in a culture of alcohol, quite the opposite, as a matter of fact. Drinking was frowned on to the extent that few in the church actually did it. Of course, being on the mission field around people from different denominations and nationalities had exposed us to enough of a drinking culture that we were not frightened off by it. Some of the Belgian missionaries we knew even ran a brewery. If this was how we could help Laura and also help calm a few people's nerves, well, who were we to refuse?

And still.

She led us down to the bar and took us behind the counter. She began pointing rapidly at things.

"There are cold beers stocked in there. If anyone wants anything stronger, let them have it. Just give them whatever they ask for, within reason, of course."

She left. Seeing that the bar was now being manned, several people dove for the counter.

"Can I have a screwdriver?" the first person asked.

Relieved that the first question was so simple, Melanie smiled confidently and pointed them down the hall toward the maintenance closet.

"Next?"

From that point on, most people asked for bottled beer. That was easy. We could handle bottles. Once we figured out where the bottle opener was, that is. It took a little searching, but with a little help from our first beer patron, we were good to go.

After a while, we got into a rhythm. We even found that a lot of people just wanted someone to talk to. To our surprise, we found ourselves in the position of, well, bartenders—part priest and part counselor. People would start with a simple comment about the streets they had maneuvered to get there, and would end up sharing about their families back home and their concerns about ever seeing them again. Even the ones who arrived at our counter clearly dealing with the stress of the situation by throwing back a few too many, basically just wanted to talk. By the end of it, Melanie and I could only shake our heads and concede that once again, God had put us exactly where He wanted us to be. Even if it was the last place two teetotalers from the Midwest ever thought they would end up.

Even so, the knowledge that our friends were still out there somewhere in the middle of everything continued to tug at the recesses of our minds. We had dozens of close Tutsi friends and so many more who were acquaintances through the church and through our basic dealings within the city. Were they safe? Had they managed to escape the aggressive Interahamwe killing mobs? I had blinked back the image of the man we had passed on the street early in our journey with the bloody stick. I had seen many more just like him walking alone and in groups on our trip to where we were now, handing out cool bottles of beer to shaken Americans. These images never left me, not even for a minute. And where were our colleagues? Every time a person would walk down the hall to where we were, both Melanie and I turned to look. Was it them? Had they made it?

Tending the bar may have been a better occupation than we had originally thought, but after a while, I was restless. I should be out there looking for them. I should be organizing other people who were better equipped to look for them. Something. I needed to be doing *something*.

So when Laura Lane walked up to the counter flanked by two Rwandese government soldiers and told us to go out and find our colleagues with them, Melanie and I couldn't toss our towels on the counter fast enough. We were out the door in under a minute.

BLIND DATE

1990
SOMEWHERE IN IOWA

As a full-timer, I worked hard in my role in Rwanda. Pastors whom I had met through my rounds with the Jesus film wrote me regularly for help with building their churches. They were responsible for purchasing land and building the walls of the church, and then I would go in and help them build the metal roofs, provided by the mission organization. As fast as the church organization was growing within Rwanda, I was in high demand. Throughout that time, I made regular treks to various building sites in order to oversee these projects. When I was finished, I would head back home to the compound I had helped build in Gisenyi.

Home.

This word was fast becoming questionable to me. Sure, I had grown up in Minnesota. My family was there. But there was something happening in me—an allegiance to another place that I had not expected. I certainly had not planned it to be so. It had sort of sneaked up on me. It was not that it supplanted my first home; it was more that it was vying for my attention as such. By now, I had gotten the earth under my fingernails. I had learned to sense the seasons. I had learned the names and voices of neighbors. I had seen faces by lamplight and risen at daybreak to the familiar song of a bird I had heard the morning before, and the morning before that. The smell of the lake now had the power to evoke memories from previous times in the same place. I had watched nightfall, seen the sun rise, and knew which way the wind would sway the clothes on the line. I had observed mothers with new babies and now, I had seen the passing of a respected friend and mentor. I do not know how else I can express the feeling in my heart about that place, apart from the word "home."

The word "home" is a slippery one for the missionary. We pack up our things, we move to where headquarters directs us, we unpack and settle in. From there, we try to find a routine. We learn where to go to mail a letter. We learn where to buy food. We learn how to pronounce and prepare vegetables we don't recognize. We learn how not to offend people with what we wear. We try and learn the culture and make friends outside of our comfort zone. We seek out others like us, too. We encourage each other through the culture shock and remind each other why we came in the first place. And then, just when we think we've got it all figured out and could actually get used to a place—the way the streets smell, the way people stand so close, the distinct absence of things like "pizza"—we pack up one more time and return to where we came from, maybe to return again, or perhaps to go on to someplace new and start the process all over again.

I cannot tell you how many times I have gathered together my clothes, my papers, and my toiletries in order to hit the road. There have been times during the breaks—the furloughs—when I've looked on people who continue to live in the same town and the same house they have always lived in with a twinge of envy. Still, if I had chosen that life, how would I know the beauty of a setting sun on a volcanic lake or the sound a golden haired monkey makes as it argues over territory? Plus, all of that moving around does serve to keep my possessions light.

By the time I came back to Rwanda this third time, I was better prepared for what I would need in order to survive in my life as a missionary on the equator. Simply put, it wasn't much. I needed a couple changes of clothes. I needed my passport. I needed pen and paper for letters home. I needed my glasses and I needed a hat. Beyond that, I would find what I needed as I needed it. Shelter was provided by the mission organization and by my own resourcefulness as a builder. Money for food and staples was essentially provided in exchange for the work by my hands and raised by the churches before I left. But there was one thing I did not have that I knew I desperately wanted, someone to love.

I was frustrated with God, I'll admit it. My friends Phil and Mimi Bjorklund who had lived and worked with me in Cyimbili had each other.

BLIND DATE

Gary and Laurie Scheer, a missionary couple who had helped me from the very beginning, had each other. In 1988, I moved to Kigali with more of a leadership role and was now living on the same compound as the Scheers, as a matter of fact. In the evenings, they frequently invited me over to their homes where we would all hang out and talk about the day's events. But at the end of the day, I thanked them and headed out to my three-bedroom house, alone. Had I not been faithful? Had I not begged God to bring me someone to share my days with? Was it so much to ask?

At the end of my four-year term, I went back to the States to do my rounds with the churches for a year. I packed up my belongings and closed up the house. On the plane, I had a little heart-to-heart with the Lord.

"OK, God. This has been a pretty tough last four years—very lonely. God, I'll come back as a missionary but you have to give me a wife. This being single is for the birds."

Now was the time for me to raise support for another four years. But I had some plans of my own. God-willing, I was going to find a wife. Little did I know, somebody else in the church had the same plans for me!

I was doing my rounds with a church in Iowa when it happened.

"So, what's the itinerary," I asked Lydia, the church secretary. Lydia was about 5'4" with a short, severe brunette bob. Thin and fit, she ran circles around the entire church staff, including the janitor and his son, who helped out during the week after soccer practice. She and I had developed a bit of a rapport over the previous week or two as we set up plans for my stay. I would drive in on Friday and leave on Monday morning, after I spoke in the Sunday evening service about my work in Rwanda. I should have known something was up by how pointedly she asked me if I was traveling alone.

"The Millers are putting you up tonight," she said, glancing sideways at me from the itinerary sheet she had neatly typed up in duplicate.

"Great," I said. "Just point me on down the road."

I was tired after having driven almost seven hours in the car that day. I had just barely caught Lydia as she was closing up the office for the weekend. She had waited around for me, this much was clear. She walked around her desk and began rapidly collecting papers and stuffing them into her topside drawer. It appeared everyone else had gone home.

"Lord knows, Alfred and I would have loved to keep you for a few days, but his mother's been having all sorts of trouble over at the nursing home, so we're barely around. Anyway, the Millers love keeping the missionaries. Greg did some mission work in Papua, New Guinea, once. I think he grew up there, as a matter of fact, long time ago."

"OK. Sounds good," I said, fighting back a yawn. I didn't mean to be rude, but I was about to drop from exhaustion. It had been a long day.

"They'll be expecting you at nine or so. But first, I have dinner lined up for you."

"Dinner? OK..."

She dropped the itinerary to her side and looked me up and down from shoes to shoulders.

"Did you bring anything a little nicer?"

"What do you mean?"

"You know, slacks? Maybe a nice button down?"

I looked at her, suddenly feeling a bit uncomfortable in my jeans and knit top. Was there a dinner party scheduled and I had forgotten about it? My mind raced back through the conversation we had had only a few days before.

"Sure, in my suitcase—"

"Fine, here," she said, thrusting the second of the two itinerary sheets into my chest. "You'll want this. Directions," she explained. "You can change in the bathroom. Just pull the front door tight before you leave." She shuffled her way noisily through the office door. "You might change your shoes, too," she called out from the front of the church before letting the door fall behind her.

Standing alone in the church, I looked down at my clothes and then down the hall toward the bathroom. Was it really necessary that I change? I looked down at the piece of paper Lydia had stuffed in my hand. It read: 6:30, 515 Maple St. #212, and was followed by some directions. I sighed deeply and headed down the hall. A nap would have to wait.

Forty-five minutes later, I pulled up outside of an apartment building. I parked and walked up the stairs to the door, realizing as I raised my hand to knock that I didn't even know who I was asking for. *Here goes*, I thought, and rapped the door twice. A young woman in her late twenties answered. She had tight strawberry blond curls all over her round head, dimpled cheeks and wore clear braces on her teeth.

"Gary Bennett?" she asked timidly, nervously tucking a short piece of hair behind an ear. She was wearing a pair of green slacks and a matching white and green striped blouse.

"I'm Gary. I guess I'm in the right place then?" I asked, laughing nervously. I loved meeting new people, but it was always a little intimidating just walking up to folks' doors whom I had never met before. "I think I'm supposed to be meeting you and your husband for supper?"

She paused awkwardly and laughed a low giggle.

"Oh, well, there's no husband here. I guess it's just you and me."

I stopped in my tracks and looked back down the hall. She *guessed*?

"My name is Celia." She held out her hand, which I took cautiously. "You can come on in. I've made us some supper."

With nowhere to run without being rude, I stepped through the doorway and followed her inside. True to her word, something that smelled a lot like a roast was in the oven. She led me into the dining room where a table was set for two. She stood staring at me, blinking like an eager puppy from the entrance to the kitchen. I noticed vaguely that her house was decorated in pastel pinks and blues with wicker baskets tucked in just about every corner. Right about then a fluffy white cat streaked past the sofa in the living room and made a bolt for the back of the apartment.

"I'll bet you're hungry," said Celia, "after that long drive and all."

"Sure," I said, not sure what else to say. She was certainly not terrible to look at—cute, even—but I had not exactly planned for this. I felt on the spot, to say the least. And she seemed, well, a little too excited to see me.

"Please, go ahead and sit down. I've made us some appetizers. I saw them do this at one of the steakhouses in town. Have you ever had a stuffed potato skin?"

I shook my head. I was admittedly a bit rusty on what was popular in the American restaurant scene.

"No, I don't believe I have."

"Well, you're going to love it."

I smiled awkwardly and pulled out one of the wicker backed chairs at the table and sat down. The table was adorned with a light blue and white striped tablecloth and I noticed that there were two forks by my plate. A small votive candle burned at the center of the table. It smelled like red hot candies.

"Lydia tells me you're a missionary to Africa," she said, returning from the kitchen with a plate filled with stuffed potato skins. I had eaten plenty of potatoes in my life, of course, but not this variety exactly. These were filled with cheddar cheese and covered in bacon bits. There was even a little dollop of sour cream in the middle. And now she was asking about missionary work. Perhaps there was some hope.

"Yeah, I am in Rwanda," I said. Even as I said it, I remembered back to the conversation I had had with God upon my return. I looked up at Celia. Was this God's plan...or was it Lydia's?

"Rwanda, wow," she said. "Do people really wear shards of bone through their ears and lips? I saw that in National Geographic. I'll bet that's amazing."

"Not exactly," I said.

"Oh, and *jambo*," she said, pausing dramatically before breaking into a grin.

"Jambo?" I asked.

"I asked someone at the church who had been there how to say 'hi' in African, and that's what they told me."

"Oh, yeah...that's Swahili. They don't speak—"

"I worked all day on that," she interrupted me with a giggle. "I even have it written down on the fridge so I wouldn't forget it. See, come here. Look."

She waved me to my feet in the middle of a bite of stuffed potato skin where I could peer into the kitchen alongside her.

"See there?" She pointed toward the fridge, a large white Whirlpool covered in cat magnets. Sure enough, a sassy Siamese wearing a graduation cap was holding up the word "Jambo!" near the handle of the freezer. We sat back down. I picked up my potato skin.

"So, you have an interest in missions?" I asked. Surely there was a reason Lydia thought I might make a good match for Celia.

"Me? Oh, no. I'm a teller at the bank. I'm not really interested in that stuff." Then, realizing she might have offended me, she quickly tried to backtrack. "I mean, I love mission work—and missionaries are great people," she said, waving her hand vaguely in my direction, "it's just I don't think I could do that. I like being able to go down the street and go to the grocery store and maybe stop at Sonic for a cherry limeade and all that. I don't know what I'd do if I had to live in a hut and eat ants for dinner and stuff."

"Ants?" I asked.

"Or grubs."

Miraculously, I made it through the rest of the evening, thanked her politely for the dinner and for introducing me to stuffed potato skins, and was on my way.

On Sunday, I spoke at the church as planned. When it was over, Celia stopped me outside the sanctuary and asked if I might like to go out for some frozen yogurt with her—an offer I declined, despite a rather pointed glance coming from the direction of one church secretary who happened to be standing within earshot. Even so, I could not lead Celia on into thinking that there might actually be something between us. We had absolutely nothing in common, and I had bigger plans. I wanted a wife, yes. But I needed the wife to want to go back with me to Rwanda. The deal I had made with God went two directions, after all. I promised I would go back *IF*.

I continued making my rounds with the churches over the course of the next few months. And when I was done, I reluctantly got back on the plane to head back over the waters—alone. There was no denying it, I was angry. I had been open to possibilities and I had tried to follow His leading. But I had been clear, had I not? I was lonely. I wanted somebody to share my life with. Here I had dedicated my life to the Lord's work, and all I asked in return was to have a partner to walk beside me. Was it so much to ask? To find somebody to love?

NO COLLEAGUE LEFT BEHIND

APRIL 9, 1994
KIGALI, RWANDA

The two soldiers followed us out to the truck in the parking lot and got in behind us, positioning themselves in the back of the cab with their AK 47s in their laps. It did not occur to us to fear them. They were government soldiers, dressed in khaki camouflage and caps. As far as we understood, they were not seeking people out to slaughter them. That was what the citizen militias were doing. Had I been thinking clearly about the Interahamwe man who threw the grenade into the house across the street from us, I might have been a little more cautious around these two. He had been wearing an official Rwanda government military jacket over his Interahamwe militia uniform and was accompanied by two government soldiers, in addition to one of his own. But surely that was not the norm. Was it?

"This is terrible what is happening," I said, glancing in the rearview mirror. I put the key in the ignition and listened to the engine roll over.

"Yes, it is," said the one sitting directly behind Melanie.

I pulled out of the driveway and turned in the direction of the district of Kicukiro.

"Is this way open?" I asked the soldiers.

"We should be all right," answered the same one who had spoken before.

Even in the midst of what I had seen, I refused to believe that this was as large as it was. Somewhere in the back of my head, I still thought that everything would blow over and get back to normal. Again, had I been thinking clearly, I would have realized the impossibility of that idea! How could a city which had seen roaming crowds of murderers going from house to house ever get back to "normal"? It defied logic. But at the time, I truly believed that we were simply in the midst of some localized fighting and unrest. We could not have known how widespread it was. We still believed that if we could just get away from the immediate fighting, we would be safe.

We were heading toward the southwest side of town on the main tar road. It was not long into the trip when I realized that where we were heading was much worse than what we had seen on the way over. There were bodies hanging half out of cars, bodies strewn across front yards. Bodies still quivering as the life seeped out of them.

"Cover your eyes," I told Melanie, time and time again.

Whereas we had seen small piles of bodies before, we saw larger ones now, stacked to almost 4 ft high at each roadblock.

There were many roadblocks.

Rwandan citizens were stopped at each one and required to present an identity card. On the identification cards there was a designation for being either Hutu or Tutsi. If their cards did not identify them as being a Hutu they would be killed on the spot. If the militiamen manning the roadblocks had any reason to believe that the ID card was a fake they had permission to kill people. We were never stopped.

We navigated our way through the streets until we arrived at the home of Larry and Diane Randolph, the first people on our list. By the looks of their street, they had not been hit nearly as hard as ours had. There were hardly any signs of fighting or terror. They met us at the door, clearly surprised to see us. It was also quite clear that they were relieved.

"The American Embassy sent us out here to get you. They're putting together a road convoy. We're evacuating."

"Well, praise the Lord," said Diane, clasping her hands together. She looked good, although unsettled, as if she had not been sleeping well.

"Are you ready to go?" Melanie asked them both.

"We need a few minutes," Larry said, also appearing as if he had been up nights like the rest of us.

"Maybe ten," interjected Diane, turning as she said it toward the hallway. "I need to finish putting away some things."

"I'll come back for you then. I'm going to get the Scheers, the Bjorklands, and the Pences," I told them, naming off some of our mutual friends. There were others on the list, as well, including a few Canadians whom I recognized. "I'll be back soon."

"See you in a few," said Melanie.

They assured us that they would be ready to go upon our return, so we climbed back into the truck with the soldiers to move on down the street. Next stop, Scott and Paula Pence. We knew the Pences, as well, having spent a great deal of time together for events associated with the church within Kigali. I parked the truck in front of their house and knocked on the gate.

There was no answer.

I knocked louder. Still no answer.

"Could you see anything?" Melanie wanted to know when I got back in the driver's seat.

"It's all quiet. They must have already left."

She was silent for a moment.

"That's good, right?"

"Well, *we* left," I reminded her.

"True. But where would they have gone?"

We pointed the truck toward the home of Laurie and Gary Scheer next. As we had done at the previous two stops, I parked on the street and went up to bang on the gate. Again, there was no answer. Melanie and I had been at that house many times and had always been met at the gate by their guard, but today, all was quiet.

"Nobody's home," I said, closing the door behind me. I gave her a brave face, but a sense of unease was gnawing at me. Melanie did not respond.

Next on the route was the home of Phil and Mimi Bjorklund. I was eager to get to them and drove as quickly as I dared. This time, a guard stuck his head out of the gate when we pulled up. I got out in order to speak with him.

"Some UN soldiers came by," he informed us. "They all went up to Don Bosco."

Don Bosco Technical School is a Catholic school for high school boys not too far up the hill from their neighborhood. I thanked him and turned back toward the truck.

"They must all be there," Melanie commented upon my reentry into the cab. She smoothed down her dress and rested her hands in her lap.

Somewhat relieved, we drove straight up to the school, which was only a few minutes away. We were surprised to find that the entrance to the campus was being guarded by several UN soldiers in camouflage and blue berets. Looking past them onto the tree-scattered grounds, we could see that there were a few cars parked near some of the buildings. Next to these was a large area filled with Rwandese people. The UN soldiers were protecting nearly 1,500 Tutsis.

A soldier raised a hand for me to stop and I pulled up beside him.

"Your name, sir?" I recognized the Belgian accent right away.

"Gary Bennett," I told him. He wrote something down on a list he held.

Just then, three men arrived at the gate beside us. One of them leaned heavily on the others and pressed a large once-white cloth to his head. Blood trickled down his face and neck.

"Please," one of his friends begged the soldier next to me in Kinyarwanda. "You must let us in. This man is hurt."

"Non," was the soldier's response in French. "Vous ne pouvez pas passez." He gestured to some of the men behind him. Two soldiers leaning against a truck stepped forward.

"Please," repeated the man's friends in Kinyarwanda. "Can't you see this man is badly injured? He may be dying. We have to get him help." All three were decidedly Hutu. There would not have been any Tutsis on the street.

"We have no help here," answered the soldiers, pressing them back as they advanced toward the entrance.

Just then, the man in the middle collapsed to the ground. I made a motion to help him when one of the soldiers in the back of my truck cleared his throat. The message was clear. I was not going to be allowed to do that. Helping this man interfered with their mission.

"You must move him away from the entrance," the UN soldiers told him. "We have orders."

The others began to argue with them, across the language barriers.

"We see the others you are protecting," the three men said in their native language. "Please, let us join them. This man needs water. He needs a doctor."

"Un médecin," added one of the men, but not able to go any further with his limited French.

The UN soldiers continued to shake their heads and pressed them farther back from the entrance.

When they had moved, the guard I had spoken to before came back to my window.

"You may come inside, but the soldiers must stay," one of the guards told me through the open window. "They are not allowed in. There will be no more Rwandese allowed in."

Concerned that the soldiers would not allow us to go in without them, I explained to the UN guard that I had been sent with the soldiers by the US Embassy. He shook his head at me.

"Sorry, sir, it is not permitted."

I translated what the UN soldier had said to me to the Rwandese soldiers.

"We need to make sure the people on this list are inside. I'll be back."

They discussed the situation briefly amongst themselves and, to my surprise, nodded. I let them out behind me. Immediately, the two friends of the injured man began to plead with the Rwandese soldiers, who spoke harshly to them in return.

"Do we look like doctors?" they asked.

The injured man sat down hard on a curb and held his bleeding head in his hands. He looked as if he would not remain conscious for long.

I pressed my eyelids at the futility of the situation. When I opened them again, the soldiers were waving us through.

Recognizing some of the vehicles in front of the chapel, a small rectangular cement building painted pale yellow with stained glass on the front, Melanie and I made a beeline toward it across the compound. When we saw Gary Scheer, Phil Bjorklund and Scott Pence all talking together in the doorway, we breathed an audible sigh of relief.

"They're here!" cried Melanie. "Thank you, Jesus."

I parked the truck next to theirs and Melanie jumped out of the truck before I even had a chance to turn off the engine. Just then Mimi and Laurie popped their heads out of the chapel, and walked briskly out to meet us. Paula Pence, too, was fast on their heels. They hugged the two of us, their eyes filled with tears.

"I can't believe you found us," Mimi said, pulling away from Melanie's shoulder, her eyes and smile glowing under her neatly combed brunette bangs. We took comfort in seeing her face. For the first time, Melanie looked as if she might cry.

We filled them in on where we had come from and how we had found them.

"And the soldiers that came with you…are they still here?" asked Phil, scratching lightly at his silvering Manhattan. His eyes were pensive through his metal-framed glasses, his cheeks ruddy from the exchange.

"They're waiting at the gate. The Belgians wouldn't let them on. Anyway, the Embassy is organizing a convoy to leave the country by ground. I was sent to get you."

The six of them exchanged glances.

"What?" I asked.

"The Belgians have already got an evacuation planned for us," Gary Scheer explained. He was wearing a simple pair of khakis and a button up shirt. His eyes were framed in glasses and his hair was brushed neatly around a slightly receding hairline. Laurie stood beside him in a simple skirt and blouse and grinned at us from beside him. She, too, looked comely and healthy and I could not help but think what a relief it was to see him and Laurie well. "See those planes?" He asked, pointing up.

I had noticed the planes circling above us, of course, but it was as if they were part of the background noise before. I looked back up at them now, realizing that they were cargo planes.

"They've been up there since we got here," Laurie said.

"And they've told you that we can get out that way? All of us?"

They nodded.

"The Belgians told us to just stay here with them and that they would get us out," said Phil.

"OK." I looked over at Melanie. "What do you think?"

She nodded back at me, "Sounds good to me."

I looked out across the parking area and located the Belgian soldiers I had spoken to before. There were others, as well, stationed at various points on the compound.

"I'll be back," I told Melanie.

I jogged over to the closest one. He looked over at me as I approached and I held out my list.

"What can you do to help find our friends?" I asked him. He looked at me blankly.

"This list was given to me by the US Embassy," I explained. "It's various American and Canadian expats who live here. I was sent to get them and have already promised that I would be back for them. Can you go get them?"

The soldier studied the list for a few moments.

"Let me go get my commander," he said.

I returned to the chapel while he went after the person in charge. After several minutes, he returned accompanied by another man who introduced himself to me as the Belgian Captain Luc Lemaire. The captain was dressed similarly in a camouflage uniform, with a blue beret on his head. His face was eroded stone, as if he had weathered many a storm in his lifetime, his mouth set in a permanent frown. Full eyebrows rose slightly at an angle outwards above his eyes. His hair was short cropped and graying.

"You want me to send my men out after some of your people?" He asked me.

"Yes, please," I told him. "I've already spoken with them. They'll be ready."

He looked out past me, scanning the perimeter as we spoke. For the duration of our conversation, he never stopped looking around us to see what was happening.

"Well, I would like to do that. We'll watch for a window and see if we can get out there. We're doing what we can with the troops we have. We are dealing with differing orders across nationalities, you understand."

"You guys are better equipped than I am," I persisted. "I've just got a truck, and a flag."

He looked out at my red, bannered truck in front of the chapel.

"Indeed, you do," he said.

"So, how about it?" I asked.

He appeared to think about it for a few seconds before meeting me in the eye.

"Ten of ours were just killed protecting the Rwandan Prime Minister," he said quietly. "Hutu forces went in and…it was severe."

The gravity of what he had told me took a few moments to sink in. This was serious. My mind raced to Mogadishu just the year before where dead American soldiers were dragged through the streets. I looked down at the sidewalk, seeing where this was going.

"I'm sorry," I said. "I hadn't heard about that yet."

"How would you?" he asked. "We're all operating on minimal communications," he said, jiggling a two-way radio in his hand.

"We've been invited by the US Embassy to join them in a road convoy out of the country," I told him, curious about his opinion on the matter.

"I wouldn't do it," he said bluntly. "We're close to the airport, we'll get you out."

"But our friends—"

"Look, we'll do what we can," he interrupted, "but what we need are more troops." He turned to leave.

Just then there was a loud commotion from the group of Tutsi people on the green surrounding some of the buildings, all rectangular and the same pale yellow as the Chapel. Outside the compound were some more shouts followed by several shots from a gun. The people in the yard were being fired on from the outside. I could hardly believe what I was seeing. Above the line of hedges around the perimeter, the head of a gunman was exposed. He wore no cap on his head and fired haphazardly toward the lawn as if he were on a wild shooting spree, aiming at nothing in particular. His teeth flashed as he grinned at his own sadistic game. The group of Tutsis ran away from the shots being fired, diving behind the buildings between them. Everything felt as if it were hanging by a thin thread. The gunmen, hovering outside the flimsy wooden fencing and lines of shrubs, could have crossed in at any time were it not for the presence of the UN soldiers. We ducked inside the chapel building as quickly as we could, gathering the children together, away from the walls. Finally it stopped, and a grave silence settled across the compound.

"What about them?" Melanie asked during the quiet.

Nobody answered right away as we weighed their uncertain fate. Our only consolation was that they were being guarded by the UN soldiers. Were it not for them, there was no question in any of our minds that they would not still be alive.

Even as I thought this, I felt my mind pushing against it. This cannot be happening, I told myself. This *cannot* be happening. I wanted to do something. At the same time, I was overwhelmed with the knowledge that there was nothing I could do. There were thousands of people armed with weapons bent on nothing less than the extermination of an entire people group. I was pinned, motionless, between the desire to help and the reality of my own futility. I felt it then, the sting of shame that comes with the realization that I would be allowed to live based on my skin color and nationality, while thousands around me would likely continue to die. I thought about our neighbors all along our street. I thought about the poor fallen people I had seen at the market and at the roadblocks, *and the dump truck.*

"Are you all right?"

I opened my eyes. It was Melanie. I could barely meet her eyes, I was so consumed with helplessness. I nodded, too overcome with emotion to answer her in that moment. We were all thinking about the Randolphs and the Fergusons, still at their homes waiting for me to come back. How could I leave them behind? What if the cargo planes circling above us landed all of a sudden and it was time to go? We could not leave them behind in the middle of the evil that had been unleashed onto the streets. At the same time, how could I risk going back out on the streets myself? What if something happened to me—who would that help? And who would take care of Melanie?

Phil suggested then that we should all pray together about what we should do. We all readily agreed. We had reached the limits of our own knowledge.

I realized then, that several hands were on my shoulders. I recognized the prayers of my friends and was suddenly flooded with a strength I did not know I had. Only moments before, I felt empty. With the voices of those dear to me, interceding for each of us and all of us—all of God's children in Rwanda—I felt it then, and I knew that God was there, even in the midst of the horror and the despair. I did not understand how or why, but it was as if His voice filled me with courage and strength.

When we were done praying, I looked around at the faces of my friends, my *family*.

"The Randolphs and the Fergusons," I paused, "Why don't I go get these guys?"

Melanie looked me in the eyes as I said it.

"Let's go," she said.

THE LIST

JULY 1990
KIGALI, RWANDA

"Come on, Gary. We know you have a list," began Laurie Scheer, looking at me kindly over a cup of tea.

I had just returned from my trip back home in the States, having raised the money needed for another four-year term, and I was complaining that I was back—still single.

Laurie was dressed conservatively, with a light pink blouse and a khaki colored skirt and wore her dark blond hair cropped short at the top of her neck and around her ears. Soft spoken by nature, she was rarely one to get into anybody's business, least of all mine. Her husband, Gary, is a deep thinker and is known as a man of prayer. He is well respected by the missionary community at large and is a great leader and teacher. Over the years I had known them, she had been nothing but respectful and hospitable to me, "the single guy." My move to Kigali from Gisenyi a couple of years before had meant that I would get to spend large amounts of time with them since we now lived on the same compound. The happy chatter of the Bjorklund and Sheer children playing together in the next room, filled the air.

"We just happen to think you should throw it out."

This comment came from Mimi Bjorklund. She and her husband Phil and I had shared a duplex in Cyimbili from 1986 to 1988. Mimi is an animated speaker who is not afraid to say what she thinks. She is also a natural entertainer. Now that the Scheers and the Bjorklunds and I all lived in Kigali, we got together regularly both for social visits and for our work.

I looked back and forth between Mimi and Laurie. We were sitting in Gary and Laurie's house at the dining room table. I was waiting for Phil to return from a meeting so that we could run a couple of errands together in town.

"What's wrong with my list?" I asked somewhat defensively. Behind me, a kitchen timer went off. The air was thick with the earthy smell of baking bread and cinnamon.

"Nothing, that's the problem," returned Mimi, jumping to her feet to pull something out of the oven. I could hear the smile in her voice. She was just getting started.

I looked across the table at Laurie, who nodded sweetly in agreement, sweetly, but directly.

"Let's see," continued Mimi from behind me as she moved about Laurie's kitchen. "You want a godly, graceful woman to marry…but she should also be from the same part of the country as you, preferably raised on a farm, have a perfect figure, and be trained as a nurse. *And* she also wants to be a missionary's wife in Africa. Oh – I think I forgot about the part about eye color. Did you want blue, green or brown, Gary?"

I glanced up at Laurie who was biting back a smile. I had been through a lot of years on the mission field with both these women and their husbands. They had become like sisters to me. They teased me like sisters, too.

"She doesn't have to be a nurse," I said, pretending to pout, "Just educated."

"Well, thank goodness for that," said Mimi. I lobbed a crumpled up napkin across the room at her.

"And you didn't have any luck back home this time?" Laurie inquired, gently.

I shook my head, uncertain about whether I wanted to tell either of them about the miserable blind date I had been on with Celia. The whole thing had been just a little humiliating and I was not quite sure if I was ready to laugh about it yet.

"Look," said Mimi, sliding back into her chair and taking hold of her teacup, "we just want the best for you. We'd like nothing more than to see God bring a woman into your life, if that's His will. We just think that you might consider relaxing your standards a bit in order to let God do His work. The woman on that list, well—she may not exist, Gary."

THE LIST

I leaned back in my seat, feeling as if I had just been punched in the gut. I knew Mimi was probably right, but how could I compromise on something as serious as finding a mate? The last thing I wanted was to find someone who I wouldn't respect and who I would feel as if I were settling for.

Laurie shifted in her seat and cleared her throat. She glanced at Mimi and the two made eye contact. It was only brief, but I had caught it.

"What?"

Laurie set down her teacup and smiled into it, swirling the hot brown liquid into a little whirlpool.

"What about Melanie?"

I laughed outright. Melanie was the young woman who had recently joined the Scheers' household in Kigali in order to teach their children. She had just graduated from college. I had met her only briefly before I left for the States and upon my return discovered that she was living on the same compound with the Scheers and me in a little apartment attached to Laurie and Gary's house. Melanie was from one of my supporting churches back home. In fact, I had stayed with her parents on one of my tours to the churches to raise support.

"What about her? She's a kid."

"She is not!" retorted Mimi.

Laurie nodded her head in agreement.

"You know I thought of her as a kid, too," she said, "but she's really not. She's a mature young woman. She and I have become good friends, you know."

"And she's beautiful. . . ," sang Mimi.

"She even comes from your neck of the woods," said Laurie.

I looked back and forth between them. This was a conspiracy.

"Hey now," I laughed. "She's too young. End of story." There was almost a twelve-year gap between us. Plus, it was quite clear that she was not looking to settle down any time soon. I knew all too well what *that* kind of girl looked like, and Melanie was not it. I thought back to Celia and shuddered.

"Remember that nurse you liked awhile back? Whatever happened there?" asked Mimi.

I groaned. Cindy was a nurse stationed in Congo. We had met up at the annual retreat at Kumbya the year before. The retreat was for missionaries all over the neighboring African countries and was a great chance to meet people. Cindy was pretty, intelligent and gregarious. There might have been something between us had I not found out after a while that she had a boyfriend waiting for her back home.

"Nothing," I said, suddenly exhausted from being the center of attention.

"All I'm saying is that we think you should give Melanie a chance. We've seen the two of you together," said Mimi.

"What do you mean?"

"Well, you two do joke a lot together," said Laurie helpfully.

"That may just be the understatement of the year," chuckled Mimi. I shot her a look. It was true that Melanie and I got along well enough. She was funny and intelligent. Since she was from the same part of the world as I, we seemed to get each other, too.

"We just think you should give her a chance," suggested Laurie.

"No. More than that," said Mimi. "If you don't give her a chance, I'm going to stop praying for you and your quest for a wife."

Laurie looked at Mimi, wide-eyed.

"Don't think I won't," Mimi said. Laurie held in a laugh with her fingers.

Just then the front door opened and a familiar face appeared in the doorway. It was Melanie. I felt my forehead go instantly hot and I stood to get myself a glass of water.

"Please tell me that you eventually get used to this sun," said Melanie. She was dressed neatly in a simple blue shirt and a long skirt that hung well below her knees. Her eyes were bright behind her glasses in spite of her complaint. Melanie had a voice which allowed her to never seem like she was complaining, even when she was.

Laurie and Mimi laughed and pulled out a chair for her.

"And look at you two. You're even drinking hot tea." Melanie shook her head in amazement. "I've been here more than half a year now and I can't do that on a day like this. I won't."

"What can we say?" asked Mimi. "You get used to it." Laurie nodded and smiled cheerfully beside her. I turned around with my glass of water and leaned against the sink.

"When did you say Phil was going to be back?" I asked Mimi again, glancing at my watch.

She smirked knowingly at me.

"I don't know, could be awhile. You know Phil—sometimes he's quick about what he's doing and other times one thing leads to another and before you know it he's balancing eight or nine projects all on top of the other. You might as well get comfortable."

Reluctantly, I made my way back to the table and sat down. Melanie looked up at me as I did so and smiled ever so slightly. Her large brown eyes looked even larger through her round glasses on her narrow, oval face. She was pretty. Even I could not deny it.

"Hi," she said.

"Hi," I answered back. I had never been nervous around her before. Normally, the two of us picked up almost a bantering type of conversational style. But the conversation we had been having before she walked into the room had gotten to me. I was frozen.

"Are you doing OK today, Melanie?" asked Laurie, breaking the ice.

"Oh yes," she said. "I was just working through some of my lesson plans. I needed a break. It's just too stuffy to be indoors. It seems better in here."

"A little," I sniffed.

"Yes, a little," she agreed. "certainly not a lot."

"Nope," I agreed. "Not a lot."

There was a pause.

"Remember those things we had as kids?" she asked. "What did we call those...a Water Wiggle? What I would give for one now—along with an endless supply of running water, of course. Oh, the things we took for granted back then."

"I think those were after my time a bit. Do you know what we called a Water Wiggle? A hose."

She smiled and took on a distant look, peering far beyond the kitchen walls.

"Ah yes, a hose. Those predated the Water Wiggle by a bit, didn't they? Turn of the twentieth century method of water transport. But by the time I was born, we had advanced considerably as humans. We even watered our crops by Water Wiggle."

Mimi hissed a laugh and stood to tend to her cake that was cooling on the counter. She began slicing big pieces of it and putting them on plates.

"That's how we watered our crops," I mumbled. Without thinking, I dipped the tips of my fingers into my water glass and flicked them up into the air. I was imagining a fleet of Water Wiggles in our hay fields back home.

"Hey," she said, "watch where you're flicking, mister." Then, following suit, she dipped her fingers in her glass and flicked them directly at me.

"Hey now!" I laughed, returning the action once again.

She took a teaspoon off the table, filled it with water and flung it at me like a catapult. I jumped to my feet just as it hit me square in the chest. Grabbing my own water glass off the table, I leaned across and poured a thin stream directly onto her head. Shrieking, she jumped up and stood opposite me at the table for protection. Wisely, Laurie inched her way out of her chair and took up a post on the other side of the room.

We paused as we considered that we were looking down the barrel of a full-fledged water war. If there were a time to stop, that would have been it. We were standing in Laurie's dining room, after all. Sure, the floor was cement and it was just water, but really. Enough was enough.

"Well, what are you waiting for?" called Mimi, "Don't just stand there— get him!"

Permission granted, Melanie reared back and threw her entire glass of water in a perfect arc over the table, landing squarely in the middle of my chest.

"Oh man," I roared, too stunned to even know what to say. Right about then, something in the back of my head clicked and I went on full autopilot. Melanie deserved payback, and if I had started it, then I would finish it. I bolted toward the kitchen sink to refill my glass, just as Mimi quickly ushered what was left of her cake and the plates into the protective custody of the oven. As I was filling it, I felt a wet smack against my back. It was Melanie, course. She had claimed Laurie's glass of water now. Twisting, I managed to dump my freshly poured glass over her brown curls as she rushed back to the other side of the table...just as Phil walked in. The two of us stood there grinning like idiots, dripping wet and squared off like a couple of young bucks.

THE LIST

"What is going on?" Phil asked, frozen in the doorway. But before anybody could answer, Melanie bolted toward the open front door. Not about to let her get away that easily, I raced after her behind one of the sheds on the compound. She was ready for me. As I popped my head around the corner, she managed to fling an entire bucket of water over my head.

For the next half hour or so, we chased, ambushed and soaked each other in what may just be the grandest water war of all times. At the end of it, when we had finally come to some sort of a stalemate under my insistence that Phil was waiting for me, I went to my house and she went to hers to dry off. As I was closing my door, I happened to peek out toward the Scheers' house next to mine. Laurie and Mimi were standing out on the front porch, both with their arms crossed over their chests and shaking their heads slowly at me.

"I don't know," Mimi said to Laurie, just loud enough for me to hear, "but I think the real question here is whether *he's* old enough for *her.*"

A DANGEROUS MISSION

APRIL 9, 1994
KIGALI, RWANDA

When I think back to how eager Melanie was to do what needed to be done, I have nothing but awe and respect for the strength she possessed. She had a strong sense that the people she loved needed help to get out of a horrifying situation, and thought nothing of her own safety. In order to help them she was ready to risk it all, having absolute faith that God would give her strength when and where she needed it.

She would tell you that what she did was only logical. Unlike the other women in our group, she did not yet have children. Anyone who has them knows that children add an entirely different dimension to the risk one places oneself in. I am certain that any of the women in our group would have volunteered to go out given a different set of circumstances, but the fact is that each of them was responsible for more lives than their own. Leaving them was not an option. That was their act of courage: to protect their families no matter what. To not only be there for them, but to be strong for them, to not turn their backs on them even for a moment, to act heroically in the face of fear for them.

Since the soldiers would not go, Melanie and I should be the ones to go back out and collect the others. It was only logical.

Only, it wasn't logical at all. How could I let Melanie back out into those streets knowing full well what awaited us on every corner? Was I going to willingly take her out into the middle of the hell that Kigali had become? Would any man take his wife out into that given a choice?

We were still newly married. We had our whole lives to live together. I had seen her eyes. I knew she wanted to go with me. But I just...couldn't.

I volunteered before anyone could argue, and I left before I could see how my leaving without her cut her to her core.

I was somewhat surprised to see that the soldiers I had left behind were still at the entrance to the Don Bosco grounds waiting for me. Perhaps I thought that they would find another way back to the main part of town. At any rate, they had stuck around to let me make good on my promise of coming back for them. They climbed into the truck once I had come to a stop, both sitting behind me in the back of the cab. I noticed vaguely that the man with the head wound and his friends were nowhere in sight.

"Let's go get the Randolphs," I told them, waving the list at them. I nodded to the Belgian soldiers guarding the gate as I said it. They returned the nod.

Retracing the streets we had come in on, we made straight for the Randolphs' house. When we were only a few blocks away, however, I heard gunfire in close proximity. Having the distinct impression that someone was shooting at us, I slowed to a stop amidst the loud cracks.

Immediately, the soldiers in the back made themselves visible, calling through the windows and making a big noise about being on official business and to let us pass. I watched the men with guns through the windows of my truck as they eyed me from behind trees and walls. It was as if they were waiting for me to do something. Run, perhaps. Had my emotions been operating at normal levels, I might have tried to make a break for it. Instead, I was still floating in the cloudy haze of shock. I was told to stop by men wielding guns, and I did.

We waited as the shooters deliberated over whether to let us pass. I could hear them, shouting back and forth to one another. I kept expecting them to approach the truck, but they never did. Nearby, I could see a shoed foot sticking out from behind a wall. The way it lay twisted revealed that its owner was no longer among the living. Sparks shot up my spine. We had driven right into the middle of a killing zone.

I continued to watch the men with guns who in return were watching us. They appeared to be debating something. One of them had a machete in one hand and a gun strapped to him, which he handled as if he might let loose with it at any given moment. When he caught me watching him, he glared at me. I looked away.

We waited several minutes as the men shouted back and forth amongst themselves.

Finally, the soldiers indicated that it was safe to advance and I inched forward until it was clear that no further shots would be fired. Once there was distance between us, I gunned the truck forward toward our destination.

When we arrived back at the Randolphs' house, Larry met us at the door. There were two small bags full and waiting at his feet.

"Are you ready?" I asked.

"We are," he said. "We'll follow you in our car up to the school."

Diane appeared behind him then, her purse slung over one shoulder.

"Have you left Melanie there with the others?" She asked.

I nodded once. She peered at me for a moment from inside the house before advancing suddenly and placing a hand on my shoulder.

"God will watch out for her, Gary."

I nodded again, a lump rising in my throat. Of course, we all knew that even as she said it, good people were being slaughtered across the city. Good people who believed in God as we did. Yes, I believed that God would protect me. I believed it stubbornly, unwaveringly. But what about the poor souls who were crying out for help and dying under the knife, the machete and the club? Many of them had believed stubbornly and unwaveringly, as well. In the end, it did not matter whether they believed in God's protection or not. Hell had been unleashed on earth and they were being swallowed by it. It made no sense. Nothing about what we were witnessing made any sense. We had no answers. We could only stand there humbly and do what we could.

I led them down a different route to avoid the place where we had been shot at only minutes before. When we arrived back at the school, the soldiers once again disembarked at the entrance upon my word that I would return to get them. The others greeted the Randolphs with a cheer and directed them to park their car next to the others in front of the chapel. The children in the group played just outside the doorway and I could see that Melanie, true to form, had organized some games for them to play. She looked up as I drove in and raised a hand to me, even as I turned around and headed back down the long driveway.

At the exit, I collected the soldiers once again and headed back down the hill.

We maneuvered our way through the streets to the neighborhood of the Fergusons.

Doris and Willard Ferguson are Quaker missionary friends of ours from Wichita, KS. Before the Fergusons came to Rwanda, they had been missionaries in Burundi for a couple of years. They should not have even been in Rwanda. They were supposed to have retired by now, but nobody could entice them to stop. Their hearts were just too big and the word "retirement" too small. If there was a need around them, they filled it, leaving little to nothing for themselves. They were well-known for running out of money at the end of the month simply because they had given away their own funds to people who needed them more.

We were farther out from the center of the city here and we saw smaller groups of people walking together now, some with wounds and others who were helping the wounded walk. Others wore the garb of the Interahamwe, the militia largely carrying out the killing campaign—kind of a loose, boldly patterned khaki. Others were local citizens, forced by the Interahamwe to kill on their behalf, or be killed themselves. Everyone we passed had a machete in their hand, every single person.

When we got to the walled entrance around the Ferguson's house, we stopped and got out. The soldiers, too, got out, opting to stay on the street outside of the gate. Their guard recognized us and let us onto the grounds before returning to talk with the soldiers.

Willard Ferguson met me in front of the house, quickly ushering me in and closing the door behind us. He is about 5'9", thin and silver-haired with a remarkable speech impediment. One-on-one, he stutters slightly, pausing sometimes before he speaks and tripping over consonants. Put him in front of an audience, however, and he speaks as fluidly as running water.

"A-ar-are you alone?" He asked right away. I explained to him that Melanie was up at Don Bosco with the others.

"I do have two Rwandese soldiers with me," I added. He narrowed his eyes slightly at the news.

Doris was wiping her hands on a towel when she appeared around the corner. As a veteran missionary, she had taken Melanie and me in the moment she met us with open arms. Doris is gentle with a short, strong build and relaxed, but kempt brownish-gray curls. A nurse by profession, she is always in a neat dress with hospitality at the ready. Any of us who has ever needed medical attention has spent time with Doris.

"I'm so glad to know you two are safe," she said. "Praise God."

"I've come to take you up to Don Bosco," I explained, filling them in on the list the Embassy had given me back at the American Club and explaining briefly how I had ended up under the protection of the Belgian UN soldiers.

"Oh…well," said Doris, her eyes flickering slightly behind her glasses. She looked at her husband.

"You say the Embassy s-sent you?" he asked, the corners of his eyes crinkling.

I nodded.

"And you want us to go with you to the American Club?" Doris wanted to know.

"No, Don Bosco."

They exchanged glances.

"Well n-now, we need to th-think this through," said Willard.

I looked at them, unable to comprehend their reluctance. Around the corner, I heard voices emanating from the kitchen.

"Who's here with you?" I asked.

"Our son and a few others," Doris answered quickly. She left the room to take care of something down the hall. Willard excused himself to join her. I could hear them discussing the situation. I sat down on a sofa and began shuffling absently through a stack of magazines on the table in front of me before leaping back to my feet and checking the window. The gate was open slightly and I could see the back of the Fergusons' guard's head as he talked with the soldiers.

After several minutes, Willard came back into the room. He had a partially packed bag in one hand. He motioned for me to sit. He took a chair opposite me and looked me squarely in the eye then.

"We have t-ten of them here," he said.

"Ten who?"

Doris sighed as she entered the room. She was carrying two folded shirts.

"Tutsis, Gary. We have ten Tutsis hiding here with us," she said.

"We won't leave them b-behind," added Willard. "We are their only hope. If we l-leave, they won't survive long. They are our friends."

I walked over to the window and looked out, uncertain how to express to them the seriousness of the situation. When the Interahamwe eventually came to the Fergusons' house—and they would eventually come there—they would not be able to protect their friends then.

"There," I said, pointing up to the sky.

"What is it?" asked Doris.

"Those are the Belgians' C-130 cargo planes. We have a seat on those. When they land, we have to be ready. They could land at any time. If we miss them, I don't know what to tell you. So, you basically have two options. Go with me now to be evacuated, or drive to the center of town to the American Club on your own to join the convoy. But for all I know, it's left by now...." I trailed off.

I thought about what Melanie would do if they landed and I was still at the Ferguson's house. She would be panicked. I would want her to go without me, but of course, I knew she wouldn't. We were running out of time.

I looked back at Doris and Willard.

"What do you think?"

"How can we leave them, Gary?" asked Doris.

Willard, too, shook his head. I sighed, desperately trying to find a solution. Suddenly, it occurred to me what we could do.

"I have an idea," I told them.

Checking the position of the guard and the two soldiers once again, I walked out the front door toward the truck, which I had parked inside their gate. The guard glanced at me with the sound of the motor, but otherwise was not interested in what I was doing. I took the truck around the side of the house to a door that was not in the direct line of sight of the driveway and got out with the engine still running. I went inside.

I found the small group of people sitting together in one of the back rooms. Several of them looked severely shaken and barely looked up at me when I entered. I explained as calmly as I could that I was going to take them to the school which was under UN protection.

"But how will we get there?" asked one of the men. "They will kill us if they catch us on the street."

A DANGEROUS MISSION

"Come look," I told him, leading him to the door. He peeked out and saw the topper on the truck with the flag.

"OK," he agreed, realizing that there was no other choice. "May God protect us."

We said a quick prayer together, all of us. Making sure that the soldiers on the street were still occupied with the guard, I opened the back of the truck and all ten of them climbed inside. When the last one was safely in, I closed the back and locked it with a padlock. The Fergusons climbed into their own car with their son and started their engine. It was time.

I pulled forward to the gate, picked up the two soldiers into my cab and waved good-bye to the guard. I could only pray that the Tutsi people in the back would not be discovered.

We drove back down the streets through mobs of bloodied men carrying *mpanga* and past several piles of the dead. I knew that if we were to be stopped and searched, we would all be killed, no questions asked. In the cab of the truck, the soldiers spoke little to each other and not at all to me. All the while, Melanie's voice echoed in my head. *It's in God's hands now.* The thought gave me strength. It kept my foot steady on the gas pedal and my eyes forward. God was watching out for us. He would protect us. I felt it in my core. We drove smoothly down the street without so much as a second glance from anybody.

At the end of the street, we noticed that a large mob had formed. The men with knives had begun chanting and singing songs and stirring themselves into yet another killing frenzy. Many of the *mpanga* they held in the air were blood-stained and I noticed then that there were women amongst them, also bearing knives. These latter ran in groups, almost as if they were stirring up the men, acting as cheerleaders of sorts. One man in the crowd bore two knives, which he held over his head. His face was stained with blood from those he had killed. He appeared to be in some sort of trance from it. As if the blood had fed his hatred and made it unstoppable. Another man near him had a knife slash across his face and across his nose, the blood trailing down his cheek and neck. As we drove near him, he flashed his eyes wide at us, exposing the parts that should have been white as a dull yellowish red. The air was thick with the intent to kill, there was no mistaking it.

The soldiers in the cab with me sensed it too and began to grow nervous themselves, looking anxiously through the windows at the hundreds of people swarming the streets around us. Surely their fate was not certain being in an American flag-bearing truck with me, by all appearances, a foreigner. We all knew enough about mobs to know that logic did not always rule the day.

Just then, one of the soldiers in the back of the cab turned around and peered in through the small window into the back of the truck at the secret Tutsi passengers! My heart sank as I saw him do it in the rearview mirror. His face transformed instantly upon the realization of whom we were transporting.

"Are you crazy?" he yelled. "You are going to get all of us killed!"

His partner turned then to look and nearly jumped out of his seat, too.

"These are Tutsi! You are transporting cockroach Tutsi!"

The two began to yell at me, demanding to know why I would put all of us in such danger.

"Don't you know this mob will kill all of us? Including us as soldiers?"

I continued to creep slowly down the street through the chanting men at close to ten miles per hour. The road was bumpy and the mob was milling around on the street. I took it slow and steadily. The sidewalks were littered with bodies, mutilated and bloody. People watched me as we passed, flashing their yellowed hate-filled eyes at me. One man held up a bloody *mpanga* and pointed it directly at me, seemingly as a warning to not stop or try to interfere.

"God will protect us," I repeated quietly several times, feeling it to be true. Outside, the chanting people parted for me as I pressed down the road.

The soldiers, however, did not agree with me and continued to escalate, threatening to throw the Tutsis in the truck to the mob. Anyone who looked into the truck would have seen their agitation. I had to do something. Finally, I reached into my pocket and pulled out a wad of the cash I had brought with me. It was from the mission's treasury.

"Relax!" I told them. "Nothing is going to happen! Take this, sit back and relax. God will protect us."

It worked. The soldiers leaned back in their seats, wide-eyed and breathing heavily, hands on their guns. A few people stepped toward our truck as we passed, eyeing the soldiers within. Pacified by the bills in their hands, their faces betrayed nothing. We wound our way down the street and out of the thick of it. Soon, we were down the road to the Don Bosco School.

When we reached the entrance, the soldiers were unwilling to get out this time. They knew full well now that the back of the truck was loaded with Tutsi people. The message was clear, if the UN soldiers wouldn't let them onto the Don Bosco compound, then I would not be allowed onto the compound either.

"You have collected all of your friends now. Our mission is done. You need to take us back to the American Club," one of the soldiers sneered.

"I'm not going back to the American Club," I told them. "I'm staying here."

I watched them in the rearview mirror, but they would not budge. I knew that the UN soldiers would not willingly let the Tutsi people in the back of my truck onto the Don Bosco campus, but the Rwandese soldiers were basically threatening to start a scene. Left without a choice, I reached once again into my pockets and pulled out some more cash.

"Here! This is more than enough to get you a ride back to the center of town," I told them.

It was acceptable. They got out. I breathed a sigh of relief and pulled up to the entrance where the UN soldiers unwittingly waived me—and ten Tutsi citizens— through. I cut through the parking lot away from where I could directly see any UN soldiers and parked by the courtyard where the others were. I walked around to the back of the truck and unlocked the padlock.

"I am going to walk away," I told them through the door. "When I am gone and it is safe to do so, get out of the truck little by little and climb the fence to join the others."

I walked away, back toward the others in my group. I never saw them leave. Later, I went back and locked up the back of my truck.

EMBERS

OCTOBER 4, 1990
KIGALI, RWANDA

The embers that ignited in April of 1994 had begun their slow burn long before the explosion of that plane.

While there had long been tensions that would occasionally flare up between the ethnic groups, much of the division that drove men to take up knives and clubs in 1994 can be traced to the 1920s when the new Belgian colonists divided and labeled the Tutsis from the Hutus, as well as a smaller ethnic group, the Twa. The Tutsis, traditionally cattle farmers who naturally drank more milk, were taller and their skulls were bigger. The Belgians brought in scientists and measured their height, the width of their noses, and the size of their brains—based solely on skull size. They were issued ethnic identity cards, stamped with the "scientific" findings from a method, which would later be used by Nazi Germans during their own killing campaigns: Hutu. Tutsi. Twa. By 1935, ethnic determination had been streamlined based on number of cattle a person owned. The ownership of more than ten cattle earned a person the stamp of "Tutsi" on their identity card, thus including any taller, wealthy Hutus who came from a cattle farming tradition.

A written history was concocted by the Belgians based on their findings, despite a lack of evidence distinguishing the groups—archeological, linguistic or otherwise. Because they were taller and lighter skinned, the Belgians believed the Tutsis had Caucasian roots and were, therefore, inherently "superior." The Roman Catholic Church at the time reinforced this distinction, developing separate educational systems for Tutsi and Hutu.

The Tutsis were allowed a voice in the country's politics while the Hutus were set to continue the farm work.

Under a Tutsi king, many Hutus became indentured servants. In the '40s and '50s, however, this practice was slowly being abolished. Cattle land was being redistributed. Hutus were gaining back power through democratic vote. A man named Grégoire Kayibanda founded the "Hutu Movement" and in 1957 wrote the Hutu Manifesto. The group slowly became militarized.

In November of 1959, Tutsis tried to assassinate Hutu leader Kayibanda and badly beat up a Hutu politician. In retaliation, Hutu militia mobilized, killing somewhere between 20,000-100,0000 Tutsis, a genocidal act that would be later remembered as the "Wind of Destruction." During this hurricane of hatred and fear, more than 150,000 Tutsis were sent off to neighboring countries. When I came to Rwanda in the 1970s, there were still whispers about what these groups had done to the Tutsis who were in power. There had been battles, riots and night raids. One rumor was that the Hutu militia had chopped off the legs of Tutsis at the knees, ostensibly "cutting them down to size."

The Tutsi refugees were collectively placed into refugee camps within the respective countries to which they escaped. In these camps, they had no rights. Their identity cards were stamped "refugee," as were their children's, as well as their grandchildren's. They would not be allowed to work or advance in society in any way. They were stuck in the camps into which they had been placed and the camps…were bursting at the seams.

In Uganda, the Tutsi refugee camps were so densely populated that people were starving and dying from malnourishment. There was no formal education. Housing was poor and subject to the elements. Cholera was rampant, with people dying en masse.

When Yoweri Museveni, a man whose sole goal was to take over political control of Uganda, approached the Tutsi refugee camps, he struck a simple deal. Give me your men to take control of my country, and I will give you mine to help you regain control of yours. Backed with the help of the men from the refugee camps, Museveni soon led a coup and took over Uganda. Established as president, he kept good on his word and on October 4th, 1990, aided Tutsi men to gain entry into Rwanda, kicking off a civil war that would lead to one of the largest genocides in history a mere three-and-a-half years later.

But while October 4th, 1990, marks the beginning of a lethal wave of destruction, it also marks the beginning of something else. For me, the night of the invasion was the night I first realized that God had not been ignoring my pleas for the previous several years. It was the night I fell in love. On the world stage, it was a small, insignificant event, this good born of destruction. For me, it was everything.

One week before the Tutsi refugee invasion, Melanie and I had gone to the American Embassy in Kigali to watch the previous week's ABC News broadcast from the States. Being somewhat starved for news from back home, this had become a habit for us. It may have been old news being a week behind, but it still seemed important somehow. It was the closest we could get, at any rate. Afterwards, we chatted about what we had learned as we walked the few blocks back home from the embassy. The sun was setting over the hills and our conversation turned to what we were going to eat that night when we got back.

"Laurie said that she was going to make a stew and that we should drop by when we get back," Melanie said.

"Sounds good! They'll want to hear an update about the war, no doubt," I said. We had all been trying to follow what was happening in the Persian Gulf War a week behind what was actually happening.

We walked down the street a ways before turning off onto the network of red stone streets leading up into our neighborhood, perched atop one of the so-called "thousand hills" of Rwanda. The sun was glowing a brilliant orange behind the lush vegetation on the path.

"Do you know what I am missing about home right now?" asked Melanie out of the blue.

"What?"

"Mexican food."

I threw my head back and laughed.

"Yeah, a big plate of enchiladas sounds pretty good right now," I agreed.

"Yes!"

I chanced a peek at her profile. We had become good friends as of late. I could feel my palms moisten a little and I stuffed my hands in my pockets thinking that it seemed warmer than usual for evening.

"Well, there's no Mexican food here," I conceded, "but there's Indian food."

"Oh yeah?" she asked, glancing sideways back at me.

"Yeah, I mean, it's not the same, but it's ... spicy."

She laughed. It was one thing I liked about her—how she laughed so freely at my jokes.

"I haven't had much in the way of Indian food," she said. "Where is it?"

"Oh, it's not too far from here. It's just across town." I swallowed. Why was my mouth so dry? "I could take you there to eat. I mean, if you want."

She smiled crookedly at me.

"You mean like a date?"

"Well, yeah. I think so. If you want it to be," I quickly added.

"I'd like that," she said after a few interminable moments. "If you think you're ready."

I looked at her.

"What do you mean?"

"Just that I've been sort of waiting for you to ask me," she grinned.

"Well, OK then."

We made our way back up the street to the compound and headed over to the Scheers' for dinner. The weekend was already booked for us, so we settled on Monday evening. Neither of us said anything to anybody right away, but by Sunday, Mimi and Laurie knew.

"Don't mess this up, Bennett," Mimi winked at me as we came out of the church. We had just been to the Kinyarwanda service at the local church where our Tutsi pastor, Prewar, had delivered a sermon about patience. Melanie was still in the church chatting with some of our Rwandese friends. She had been learning the language through her tutor far faster than I ever did.

"There's nothing to mess up," I said, trying to act casually. My friend, Alexi, was waiting to talk to me over by the edge of the street. He was in the process of becoming a pastor of his own church and had taken me on as sort of a mentor in the process. He and his family had never been anything but warm and friendly to me. I waved over to him to indicate to Mimi that I had no time to discuss the situation. As I walked over to meet him, I could hear her chuckling with Laurie and Phil behind me.

When Monday finally came, my stomach was in a knot. What if the date went poorly? What if the date went well? Was I really prepared to pursue a relationship with Melanie? Did I really want to set myself up for that kind of disappointment? The age difference felt enormous. And yet, when we were together, it was as if it did not exist. I had to continually repeat this latter over and over to myself. I could not deny it—our friendship just felt…right.

I have never been one to anguish over clothing or my appearance. Even so, that day I made sure that I had a clean shirt and pants ready to go. Thinking back to my strange meeting with Lydia, the church secretary from Iowa on a mission, I even made sure that I wore my Sunday shoes. I wanted to look sharp, polished.

So when I heard news through the grapevine that a curfew had been set for all of Kigali that night, I could not really understand what I was hearing. I asked around and sure enough, Kigali was to be closed up tight at sunset. Nobody was allowed out on the streets. I was stymied! As long as I had been living in Rwanda, this had never happened before. Surely it was not a sign. Could it be a sign? Awkwardly, I headed over to Melanie's door.

"What does that mean, a curfew?" she asked, narrowing her eyes at me after I told her what I had heard. "We're not going to be back that late, I imagine. Who gave us a curfew? I really don't think the Scheers are going to mind."

"No, no, not that kind of curfew," I explained. "The entire city is under curfew. There is something about refugees trying to cross the border. It doesn't really make any sense," I admitted, shaking my head.

"Refugees are trying to cross the border?" asked Melanie pursing her lips, clearly unimpressed.

"I know. It sounds weird. I'm not sure what in the world is going on."

She crossed her arms over her chest and leaned one hip on the doorpost.

"OK, well, I guess we're just going to have to take a rain check."

"Absolutely," I gushed a little too readily. "This isn't over. I've got to take you to try the Indian food."

She smiled, sort of a half-smile mixed with a healthy dose of incredulity. "Sure," she said. "We'll get to it."

"Hey now," I said, "I'm really not making this up. We're really not allowed to go out to eat tonight."

"OK," she said, shrugging. "I'll be seeing you." She took a step back.

"There really is a…"

She smiled at me and shut the door.

"…curfew," I said.

I spun around and looked out over the grounds for a moment. OK, I thought. That didn't go so well.

The next day, I was walking across the compound when Melanie came trotting up beside me.

"OK, I owe you an apology," she said. I was heading toward my wood shop to do a little work on a shelf I was trying to finish. I glanced at her.

"What for?"

"For not believing you yesterday… about the curfew."

"It's OK," I shrugged. I stopped then and looked at her. She stopped, too.

"Indian food." It was all I could get out.

"Right. Indian food." she repeated.

We smiled dumbly at each other for a few seconds before making our excuses and parting ways once again, she off to the shed she had converted into a schoolroom for the children, and I off to my wood shop. I had wanted to go ahead and suggest a different night that week, but when I discovered that the curfew was still in effect, I decided to wait and see what would happen. Three days later, I was still waiting. The curfew had not yet been lifted.

I was sound asleep on the night of October 4th when it started. I was alone in my house in Kigali on the same compound with Gary and Laurie Scheer and Melanie was in the guest apartment. I was abruptly awakened to an explosion of sound. Forced upright with the rush of adrenalin, I froze in the dark, trying to make sense out of what I was hearing. What was that sound? Firecrackers? I glanced at the clock. 2 a.m.

When the noises continued, escalating with each passing moment, I forced my feet to the floor and peered out the window. Outside it was dark and still, but the noise kept coming in waves of thunderous cracks. It was at about this point when I realized I was hearing gunfire, but where? Why? I was not aware that there that there were that many bullets in the whole country—let alone an arsenal of weapons that would supply this thunder. And furthermore, what was happening? Were we at war? I knew that the United States was at war in Iraq. But why would that carry over here, in the middle of the African continent? Having been only recently jarred from my sleep, it didn't make sense. Then it came back to me, all of the news about the refugees invading Rwanda, and the nightly curfews. Did the refugees have guns? I pictured groups of people who had been living outside the country trying to sneak across the border with their families. But why did they have to sneak in the first place? The borders were more or less open. And why would they need guns? It wasn't making sense. I stood rigid at the vibrating window staring out into the impenetrable dark.

When a knock came at the door, I almost missed it in the midst of the other noise. I grabbed the clothes I had worn earlier that day off the back of the chair on which they had landed.

"Coming!" I called, half hopping to the door while I pulled them on and expecting it to be Gary Scheer next door. When I opened it, Melanie was standing on my doorstep dressed in a T-shirt and sweat pants. Her arms were crossed tightly over her chest. My heart did a little skip.

"Gary? What's going on?" She asked, her face twisted with concern.

"I have no idea, but I don't think you should be standing out there." I laughed nervously over the continuing noise in the background.

She glanced over her shoulder and stepped into the living room. I closed the door behind her and walked briskly to the window to peek out through the curtains again. All I could see was a darkened Kigali, but the sound continued to echo all around.

"This is crazy," I said.

"You're not kidding. Sorry to end up here. I tried knocking on the Scheers' door, but I guess they couldn't hear me over the noise. I was afraid to yell. I didn't want to wake up the children." She paused for moment before laughing, "I guess that's a little silly, considering." I sniffed a laugh, too.

"Have you tried the radio?" She asked, peeking out the opposite side of the curtain.

"I don't think any of the stations are up and running...."

Even so, I retrieved it from my bedroom and turned it on, searching for a station and, as predicted, not finding one. Everything was shut off for the night and no one was reporting. It was dark in the house and I suddenly felt a surge of concern that it might be improper for the two of us to be alone in the middle of the night in my house with the lights off.

"I would turn the lights on, but—"

"Oh, for goodness sake, Gary," she said, "I'm not concerned about my reputation! Considering the circumstances, turning on the lights might be just about the stupidest thing we could possibly do."

"Absolutely," I agreed, turning back to the window. She did the same. We looked out into the darkness in silence, separated by a few feet and a curtain. Staring out through the pane together seemed intimate somehow. After listening together for close to a minute, she spoke up.

"So, I guess this is why no Indian food?"

I looked at her. She was smiling.

"Hm. It would appear to be so."

"It will just have to wait then."

"It will," I answered.

"But not too long," she added.

"No. Not too long."

"Still not Mexican food, but it will have to do."

"Yes," I said.

"And it will do just fine," she said.

I looked over at her face in the shadows, watching me from the windowpane side of the curtain. A little cloud of breath had fogged up the window in front of her mouth. It felt like we were in our own private booth. I wanted to reach out to her—take her hand, put my arm around her and tell her that everything would be all right—but I did not dare. It was too early. We hadn't even had Indian food yet.

"It will do just fine," I repeated, distantly. I felt my neck go hot as we stared into each other's eyes.

She smiled first, breaking the spell of the moment.

"Well," she said, popping back out to the room side of the curtain as if we were discussing the price of yams at the market. "We don't know what's going on, but thank the Lord that He does. We just have to trust Him that everything is going to be OK."

I nodded, suddenly unable to speak.

"Should we maybe head over to Gary and Laurie's now?" she asked gently. "There's no way the kiddos are still asleep anymore."

"Yeah," I agreed. "Whatever is happening out there, it looks like Kigali could use some prayer. Let's go."

NIGHT

APRIL 9, 1994
KIGALI, RWANDA

I lay awake in the dark, the sound of shifting bodies and heavy breathing all around. Beneath me, the cement floor relentlessly pressed into my hip and turned it numb. I shifted to my other side, away from Melanie, asleep with her head on her bag. I peered into the dark above the backless wooden benches where some of the others slept on the perimeter beside me and allowed my eyes to be drawn toward the darkened stained glass windows at the front of the chapel. On my side of the windows, close to fifty people lay in various stages of sleep: Belgians, Italians, Americans, and Rwandans lucky enough to be married to an expatriate. Outside those windows, approximately 1,500 Tutsis slept on the grass in the tree lined space across the lot from us. Earlier in the night, the mob that waited outside the grounds with guns and knives had fired in at the sleeping masses. There had been sounds of whispered surprise, muffled panic. And then back to silence.

We slept, of course, without any light. Not even the light from a watch was allowed. The men who circled like wolves outside the compound hurling insults within would have nothing to shoot at.

There still had been no word from the Muellers, the missionary family who had only been in Rwanda for nine months. Earlier that afternoon once the Fergusons had joined us, I went down to talk to some of the soldiers. I wanted news about what was happening. Having almost been caught in that mob on my last mission out, I was concerned about how we would transport the Muellers safely to where we were. We needed to get them out, but how would we do it in a way that would not cause greater risk to them? I had seen the faces of the killers, their eyes cold and their bodies worked into a frenzy. There was no logic left to them. It was as if they were possessed. They were only on Day 3 of what would later become known as One Hundred Days of Killing.

Of course, I could not know this at the time. All I knew was that they had lost all capacity for compassion or love. They had been taken over by hate and fear and had lost their humanity in the process. I also knew that driving through them again in my flag adorned truck would likely end badly.

Earlier that afternoon, I had excused myself from our friends to retrieve my car from where I had parked it. The back was empty, as I knew it would be. I assumed they climbed the fence to join the others, but really, I have no idea where they went. Perhaps they did, perhaps they didn't.

On my way back, I swung down to where there was a cluster of Belgian soldiers. I figured I would make one more plea to them to see if they would go collect the Muellers. I had already asked them a couple of times before, and each time I had been assured that they would do it just as soon as they had the chance. The day was slipping by fast, though. Before long, it would be dark.

I found them huddled around a battery-powered television. It was in French, but the pictures spoke for themselves as reporters shot angle after angle of the mass destruction. There were thousands dead, cut down and left where they lay. Outside of houses, in roads, in earth pits. My stomach sickened at the sight of it. Of course, I had seen it with my own eyes, but now it was different, ironically made more real through the lens of television.

"Please," I said to Captain Lemaire when I finally tracked him down again, "Please send some troops out after our people. They're not going to make it out of this without your help. They have children."

He didn't say anything.

"You're not going to go out after them then, are you?" I questioned him, my voice lowered so the others would not hear. His eyes held mine steadily as he spoke.

"Frankly," he said, "I value the lives of my soldiers too much to send them out there. We're not doing any more rescue missions." He turned to leave.

"OK then," I told his back. "I'll go."

NIGHT

He whirled around and looked at me, a sneer in the corner of his mouth.

"I wouldn't send my men out there into this without an armored vehicle at the very least!"

I nodded, realizing at that point there was nothing we could do. Night was coming fast. If I went out after them, we might all be killed. I could only pray that they would be safe if they just stayed put. And still, it was possible that they had found another way out. Problem was, we just didn't know.

The Belgian soldiers gave us MREs, or army rations. Many of us, grateful as we were, were surprised by the thought of food after a full day of going without, and could only stare at the bits of bagged sloppy chicken stew, smoky franks or omelets with ham and wonder how such items might be consumed. The children among us went straight for the crackers with spreads or dessert bars, and we quickly found that they were onto something. Food just seemed so out of place, irrelevant, even. We ate what we could stomach.

We had been given bottles of water, as well. These seemed more useful and necessary. Our bodies welcomed these without hesitation. For many of us, this was the first water we had even thought to drink all day. Those bottles were life.

When the sun went down around 6 o'clock, we began settling into our places. The UN soldiers had warned us to be quiet and that we should not make any noise for the same reason we should not have light. They did not have to ask twice. We had all seen and heard the mob chanting death beyond the back of the property. They also instructed us to sleep with our shoes on. Our vehicles remained in a semicircle facing outwards with the keys in the ignition just outside the chapel door in case we had to move quickly.

Awake now half a night later, I looked around the chapel wondering what it was that had stirred me from my sleep. Granted, sleeping on cement is not exactly conducive to deep slumber, but I couldn't help but feel as if I had heard something. There had been gunfire both nearby and in the distance throughout the night. But that's not what I heard. This was different.

My ears strained in the dark. Throughout the night, I had heard the muffled sobs from one Belgian man's Tutsi wife. We all knew the story. At her request, she had pleaded with him to drive by her family's house in order to pick them up and take them to Don Bosco with them. Upon their arrival, they found them dead—adults and children—in the front yard. She was consumed with grief. We could only sit helplessly by, able to offer no comfort.

Was it she whom I had heard?

I wasn't certain, but when nothing else presented itself, I finally willed my eyes closed and tried to go back to sleep. When I heard a loud WHAM several eventless minutes later, I sat bolt upright.

All around me was a pause—and then the loudest, most blood-curdling wail imaginable. It took several seconds to register it. It was one of the children. One of the children was hurt!

Chaos followed as adults made their way on hands and knees toward the screaming child. It was Zachary Pence, I realized after a few seconds. Paula, his mother, was already holding him. *It's OK,* she whispered in the dark when he paused to gather more breath. *He hit his head on the table when he sat up. It's OK. It's OK.*

She held him tightly to her chest trying to absorb his sound into her. The door at the front of the chapel swung wide and one of the soldiers came into the room.

"Somebody shut that kid up!" he whispered sharply.

Young Zachary, fearing the soldier, only escalated his wailing. In the dark, his mother rocked and rocked.

THE BEGINNING

APRIL 7, 1991
KIGALI, RWANDA

On the day I asked Melanie to marry me, I rose early. Through my window, I could see that the sun was just a yellow glow over the horizon. The birds were only starting to stir.

I could hear Homer moving around, so I pulled on my clothes and went to join him. Homer and I had been sharing my big house on the compound for some time now as he had continued to help out with the various construction needs of the mission. As he had done so many years before back in Gisenyi, Homer remained a close friend and mentor.

I found him in the kitchen, standing in front of the coffee maker and staring intently at it as it popped, sizzled and slurped its way to completion. He was already dressed for church in a pair of dark gray trousers and a light blue button down shirt. An empty coffee mug stood at the ready on the counter.

"You know you don't have to wait for that thing to stop," I told him. "It has a trigger that stops the flow when you pull out the pitcher."

"Yeah, I know," he said good-naturedly without turning around, "I don't mind waiting for it to come to completion."

I shook my head and bit back a smile. I knew Homer well enough at that point to know that there was a kernel of wisdom tucked into his simple statement.

"And I am sure of this, that he who began a good work in you will bring it to completion at the day of Jesus Christ," I said, quoting the verse from the first chapter of Philippians. It was a good reminder to be patient to see the fruits of our labor in the Lord.

"There's that, yes. But also I like to turn the burner off right away so it doesn't get bitter. If I pull a first cup out before it's done, I often forget to do that." He tapped his head a couple of times and winked at me. "Think tank's not quite as reliable as it used to be."

"Nothing wrong with your think tank," I muttered, laughing.

"What's that?" he asked.

"Nothing."

I walked over to the toaster and popped in a couple slices of bread.

"I was thinking of making a stew for us for after church. Maybe invite a few folks. Are you going to be here?" Homer asked.

"Ah, thanks for the thought, but I think I've got plans today," I told him.

He turned to glance at me.

"You *think*?"

"Yeah."

This time he faced me square. I smiled and looked down at the toaster.

"I'm thinking of asking her to marry me today."

"Well," he said, sniffing and momentarily forgetting what he was doing. A slow smile spread across his face as he processed what I told him.

Certainly there should not have been any real surprise in what I was telling him. It seemed everyone knew we had become an item. Only a few months before, it had practically been broadcast across the entire African missionary community.

We had been attending an annual multi-country missions conference at Kumbya, one of the peninsulas along Lake Kivu. More than 200 missionaries were there from several of the African countries: Uganda, Congo, Burundi, and many more. During the day we attended services and sessions before splitting off into free time, frequently doing things like water skiing and playing games. I drove the boat E.J. had made and pulled whoever wanted to give it a try behind. Melanie, of course, wanted to take a crack at it, so I willingly towed her until she crashed and I pulled her up from the water, laughing all the while. Something about the way we looked at each other and interacted tickled the fancy of several of the younger kids, leading them to commence a multi-day teasing campaign involving loud, playful sighs and aggravatingly well-placed public commentary like, "Aw, look at the lovebirds" or "You two are *maaade* for each other," throughout the retreat.

At night, those of us who were single generally hung out together, laughing and playing card games like "Spoons" well into the night by the light of kerosene lamp. The ratio of men to women was noticeably off-kilter, leading many of my married friends to tease me about "Gary and his harem," but I shrugged it off. There was only one girl in the group I had my eyes on. Anyone who didn't know it had, quite simply, not been paying attention.

Homer looked up at me from the hissing coffee pot. "That's fantastic."
"You think that's a good decision?"
"I think that's a great decision." His eyes began to shimmer wet.
"Yeah?"
"Yeah."
He placed a well-worn hand on my shoulder; looked me in the eyes.
"I wish you guys the very best."

We chatted for a while as he began taking potatoes out from the fridge to peel and cube for his stew. He seemed genuinely happy for us. Giddy, even. It felt good to get his blessing. He was one of those people whose opinion mattered to me. He was wise and I respected him.

Collecting my toast and coffee, I sat down at the table. In my pocket was a letter from another man whose opinion mattered to me: Melanie's father. I had written him a month or so before to ask his blessing on his daughter's hand. To be honest, I was not exactly sure what he would say. Just that Christmas, Melanie's mother, Marcia, had come to Rwanda for a visit. Since I had a car and Melanie did not, I ended up being drafted to drive them around to do some sightseeing. I took them down to Butare to see the museum and even out to Cyimbili to see the Bjorklunds and to spend Christmas out there with them. It was on one of these trips that I first posed the question regarding Melanie and me.

"So, Melanie and I are starting to get serious," I told her, broaching the subject somewhat cautiously.

She was sitting beside me in the passenger seat.

"Well, I know you are," she began. "And you two seem to get on well enough. It's just that, to be perfectly honest, I worry about the age difference between you two. If you were to marry, chances are Melanie would spend a lot of years as a widow," she said.

I nodded at what she was saying. The twelve years between us was a concern of mine, too. Even so, try as I did I could never seem to reconcile this logic with the reality of how well we connected. It just did not seem like it was ever actually a big deal. It certainly was not to Melanie. Even our closest friends said that it was as if it were not even there. But her family was a different story. That conversation with Marcia was telling. So, when Melanie's father wrote back saying that he would be honored to have me as his son-in-law, I could hardly even believe it. At that point, there was nowhere to go but forward.

Pushing my plate of toast back onto the table a ways, I pulled a card out of my breast pocket and set it down in front of me. In my pocket was a ballpoint pen. I retrieved it and clicked it into readiness. As it hovered over the paper, I hesitated. There was so much to say. How could I possibly write it all? I didn't want to sound trite or syrupy.

I took a sip of coffee. Set the mug back down. Sighed.

"Will you marry me?" I finally wrote, flourishing the question mark at the end a little more than I had intended. It was quick and to the point. It would have to do.

I headed off to church with Homer soon after that. Melanie had caught a ride with the Scheers, so I waited until the service was just about to begin to ask her. We were sitting in a backless pew with our feet resting on the dirt floor of the Rwandan church service we went to. Prewar, our pastor, was sitting at the side of the church, looking over some of his notes. Both Rwandese and American missionaries were still coming in through the entrance at the back of the small church. I leaned over to her.

"Want to go to lunch after church?" I asked.

She shrugged casually, but I could see by her expression that she was pleased.

"Sure."

"There's a place I want to take you."

"All right," she said, giving me a quick pat with the back of her hand on the side of the leg. As we were in public, she would not have dared to do more than that. Rwandese culture did not look fondly on any sign of affection in public, including something as benign as handholding. Now, had she been a man, we could have held hands all day long as a sign of our friendship. But the fact was, she was a woman and I was a man. There were rules that had to be strictly followed.

When church was over, Homer assured me that he had found a ride back with a couple of the people he had invited over for stew and I took off with Melanie. In the car, she turned to me.

"So, where are we going?"

I bounced my eyebrows mysteriously.

"You'll see."

"Oh," she sang. "Somewhere fancy, is it?"

When I didn't answer, she looked at me.

"Is it?"

I laughed.

"Maybe."

I drove her to a hill at the center of the city and began making our way up the road to the top.

"You're not taking me to the President's Restaurant, are you?"

I grinned.

"Well," she said in mock surprise. I could see her gears turning, but she didn't say anything.

I parked the truck in a small area for cars and walked around the truck to open the door for her.

"This is some treatment," she said. "Be careful. A girl could get used to this."

Inside the restaurant, I requested a table out on the balcony overlooking the city. The server led us through tables filled with diners through a door to a small round table covered in a white cloth. In the center of the table was a small, tasteful arrangement of local flowers.

"Now, what shall we have?" I asked, looking over the menu as if it were no big deal that I had taken her to the nicest restaurant in all of Kigali.

She let out a low whistle.

"Soup?" she asked, a bit taken aback by the prices.

"How about a steak?" I suggested.

She looked at me, obviously amused.

"What's all this about?"

"What's all what about?" I returned.

She shook her head and covered her face with her menu. I knew she suspected what was up, but she was doing such an excellent job pretending like she didn't that I didn't want to blow her cover. Besides, I was having fun watching her squirm.

We ordered steaks and salads and chatted about our life in Rwanda. Below us, the city shimmered with life. Nothing bad was happening that day. Nothing bad *could* happen that day. When we were finished, our server brought us dessert menus and we ordered something chocolate to share. She brought us the dessert with two spoons soon after and we began chipping happily away at the cake and cream. When we were halfway through, I realized that I couldn't wait any longer. I dug in my pocket and pulled out the card.

"Melanie, I—" I stopped, realizing somewhere in the back of my mind that everything I said would be remembered and that it was important that I got it right. I hesitated, suddenly afraid to proceed. She reached out and gently put her hand on top of mine across the top of the table—an action both of us knew was pushing the borders of propriety in Rwandese culture. I looked up at her and smiled, regaining my voice.

"I didn't think you were real," I began, the words coming out more quietly than I had intended. She looked at me, confusion knitting together her eyebrows. I backpedaled. "I mean, of course I knew you were real, but all this time I've carried around this list. The things I knew I wanted to find in a woman—in the woman I want to be with—and here you are. How can I not know that God sent you to me?"

She smiled broadly.

"And you to me."

"I want you to be happy. I want us to be happy. And you know I don't have a lot of means. I'm a missionary. Well, you understand. I guess you know who and what I am by now."

"And I love who you are," she said quietly. "I love everything about you."

I shook my head and sniffed a laugh. I could hardly believe how blessed I was. How could I have found a woman who fit so perfectly with me—who accepted my faults along with everything else? Slowly, I rose to my feet and

THE BEGINNING

scooted my way around the table until I stood before her. I dropped to one knee and took her hand. She was smiling, covering her mouth slightly with one hand and looking as if she might cry. I handed her the card. She read it and choked out a laugh.

"Will you?" I asked, realizing that I really hadn't needed the card and wanting to make sure she heard it from my own mouth. "Will you be my wife?"

She threw her arms around my neck.

"Yes," she said in my ear. "I'll marry you."

I was so happy that I hugged her back, not caring in the slightest about who saw us. A few people on the balcony had been watching us and began clapping. We pulled away from each other, slightly embarrassed.

We finished our dessert soon after and left the restaurant, taking our time as we walked to the truck. Next to the President's Restaurant were a number of grass huts constructed as replicas of the traditional Rwandan grass hut. Different parts of the country constructed their homes a little bit differently, and several were represented here. Hidden by the huts from the road, I reached down and took the back of her head in my hand. I pulled her gently toward me and kissed her.

"I love you," she said.

Inspired, I swept her up in my arms and carried her over to the entrance of one of the huts as if I were carrying her over the so-called threshold.

"I promise to do at least this well for you," I teased, looking up at the inside of the hut.

In my arms, she leaned her head into my chest and joked sweetly back, "You'd better."

MY HIDING PLACE

APRIL 10, 1994
KIGALI, RWANDA

When Sunday morning came, most of us were awake before the sun. Cautiously, we emerged from the chapel, standing by the doors and looking around in an attempt to assess whether anything had changed during the night. In front of us, our cars remained at the ready. To our left, the large group of people was still there. Many of them were standing on the grass now, having slept all night out there on the damp green. Above us, we could still see the cargo planes circling through the clouds. Around us, armed Belgian UN soldiers stood watch over the grounds. And on the street, the men with weapons waited.

We did the best we could to make things appear normal. We did this not only for ourselves, but also for the kids. There were nearly ten children amongst us. Melanie and the other women tried to organize games to keep them occupied and close to the chapel. They played Duck Duck Goose, Bible Quiz games, Charades, etc. Even so, it is impossible to keep children completely occupied for an entire day. There were long periods where they would simply play together and lose track of where we were and the seriousness that surrounded us. For the most part, this was a blessing, for all of us.

"You kids stay between the building and the cars," Melanie called out to the kids once the sun was up and the children were in full swing. A few of the children were too young to be able to effectively follow instructions. Even so, Melanie was in her element and she and their mothers had managed to organize them into a game of silent Freeze Tag. If someone made a noise, they had to freeze same as if they had been tagged.

"These cars?" asked one of the boys. He was three, maybe four, and named Brian. It was one of the Pences' kids, notorious for his love of freedom in the outdoors. He had already been redirected and chased back to the door by his own mother and father several times.

"Yes, those cars," Mrs. Pence answered him, shaking her head. "Always pushing his borders," she said to Melanie.

"You older ones are going to have to help keep watch," Melanie said, turning to a couple of the others. "It's dangerous out past the cars."

"Why?" It was Brian Pence again, already on his way to the boundary Melanie had just set. He paused, his proverbial big hairy toe hovering over the line.

Melanie paused for a moment. "Because there are angry people out there. We have to stay here behind the cars to be safe."

She had all of the kids' attention now at the mention of the "angry people."

"Are they going to hurt us?" asked one of the girls. It was Leah Bjorklund, shy and cute as a button with blond hair.

"No, sweetheart," Melanie said exchanging glances with Mimi. "God's not going to let that happen."

"What about the other people?" Leah asked. Melanie bent a knee and got low to the ground.

"What other people, honey?"

"The other people that already got dead. Mommy and Daddy said there were people who got dead on the way to the church. "Why did God let that happen?"

Melanie looked up at me over her shoulder.

"Oh sweetheart, I don't have the answer. But God is with us even when things go bad. He is our hiding place where we can go when we're scared and He keeps us brave and safe in His love. Does that make sense at all?"

The little girl nodded.

"Maybe the people who got dead, got dead in God's arms. And then He picked them up and told them they could live with Him."

Melanie's eyes welled up with tears and she hugged the little girl tight.

"Maybe it was just like that."

It was soon after that when we decided to hold an impromptu service in the chapel. We prayed, sang and found comfort in one another and in God's word. We read Psalm 32:7. "You are my hiding place; You will protect me from trouble and surround me with songs of deliverance." For many of us who were frightened, this gave us strength. We thought about how no matter what happens—come fear or attack or even death—we could trust God to protect us. People could destroy our bodies, but our souls would be secure, safely hidden in His peace. What a radical thought in the midst of what was happening outside our gates.

Together we sang the words [1]:

You are my hiding place
You always fill my heart
With songs of deliverance
Whenever I am afraid
I will trust in You

I will trust in You
Let the weak say
I am strong
In the strength of the Lord
You are my hiding place...

(Selah)

It gave us peace in those hours of uncertainty. Even in the midst of death, of angry people bearing knives, machetes and guns hurling awful words of hate into the compound where we all were, we felt God's presence. I am not sure I would have found it possible had I not lived through it, but it was unmistakable. God was there.

When we were done, the group within the chapel slowly dispersed. Some of us wanted to sit quietly while others wanted to go outside to get some fresh air. Still others of us had different ideas of what to do. Willard

---

1   *Music by Michael Ledner from Psalm 32:7)

Ferguson and Gary Scheer went to the fence separating the Tutsis from us and talked and prayed with many who were there. Before long, we heard the sweet sound of song coming from the grassy area.

"I can't even imagine what they must be going through," Melanie said quietly to me. We were standing at the chapel door, her head leaning against my shoulder.

I nodded vaguely. Part of my own way of dealing with the horror of what was happening around us was to shut down my feelings and emotions. One man in the crowd I had even recognized from my dealings around the city. He was a clearing agent at one of the customs agencies. We had a very good working relationship. I should have said something to him. I should have acknowledged him. Instead, I am ashamed to say that I could not bring myself to do it. I was too separated from myself to think about what anyone else was feeling. It surprised me that Melanie could.

"I only pray that God will forgive them," she added.

I looked at her, realizing for the first time that she was speaking about the people on the street who were doing the killing. A lump rose in my throat, past the block in my emotions. I realized then that not every emotion I felt was being suppressed. Unlike Melanie, though, I was not feeling compassion toward those men in that moment. The images of the poor slain bodies on the street were too fresh in my mind. What I was feeling... was anger.

"Help me, Lord," I whispered.

Shortly after, the UN soldiers gathered us together to update us on what was happening.

"The planes are still looking for a time and a place where it is safe to land," they told us. "Be ready to go at any time."

Each of us was assigned a car and given a number. We had our bags zipped and ready to go at a moment's notice. At times, it seemed like they might call us any second. And still, time spiraled on.

Meanwhile, on the street, the crowd outside the Don Bosco School only grew thicker. They yelled at the people who had taken refuge within, threatening rape for the women and dismemberment and death for all. Gunfire could be heard frequently on the street, along with chanting calling for the death of the "Tutsi cockroaches."

MY HIDING PLACE

The Tutsi people were visibly unnerved. Many stood together, holding each other and crying openly. Others were stoic and serene. No matter how they dealt with it, though, they all knew that the only thing that stood between them and the evil outside the gates were the UN Soldiers.

Of course, they did not know about the ten Belgian soldiers who had already been killed. They had no television or radio communications amongst themselves. If the men were able to force their way in, taking out the soldiers as they came, there would be no stopping them. They would kill all of us. There would be no one left alive!

Staying between the cars and the chapel, we watched and we prayed. We had no choice but to trust in God for strength. Wherever the Muellers were, we had to believe they were in God's hands, as were we.

Late in the morning, a high-ranking soldier from the former government showed up. I recognized him, but of course did not know him. While he was talking, I went across the lot to talk to his chauffeur, thinking I might be able to get some information about what was happening in the city. He glanced at me as I approached him, before quickly looking away.

I placed a hand on the top of the car and leaned down to better talk to him.

"Amakaru?" I asked. *What is the news?*

He shrugged and stared straight ahead, lips closed and hands on the steering wheel, an action I considered unusual in the face of what was happening. I had never met a Rwandan before who was not immediately welcoming and willing to chat.

"Things are pretty bad out there," I prompted him through the window. He made no move to exit the vehicle or to face me.

"Yeah, they're bad," he answered, finally, exhaling deeply.

I stood there a few moments longer as the driver continued to stare steadily out the window in front of him. When he said nothing more, I tapped the roof of the car.

"Right. Well, take care," I said. I headed back to the others contemplating the driver's behavior. Why wouldn't he talk to me? It seemed so odd.

Just then, I noticed a man walking up the driveway toward us. He was a white man, which right away I thought was strange—and by all practical appearances, alone and on foot.

I squinted to get a better look at him and began toward him, meeting him in the driveway. I soon recognized him. It was Verne DeMille—one of the Canadians on my list. He was a missionary, like us.

"I don't believe it," I said, holding out a hand to him. He took it.

"I'm glad to find you still here," he said. "The American Embassy sent me out after you."

I blinked at him incredulously.

"What? How did you get here? Did you walk the whole way?"

"No, no. They gave me a car. I left it at the gate." Verne pointed with his thumb.

"But... how?" I asked, wondering at the danger the streets had descended into. Not even the soldiers were going out.

"I have no idea," he said, shaking his head. "All I can say is they're clearly not after me. They had their chance."

"Well, what in the world are you doing here? Why did the American Embassy send you?"

"To find out if you are you planning on joining the road convoy," He answered.

"They haven't left yet? We've decided to stay here and try to get out via the airport. We're taken care of here," I told him.

"Well," he said, scratching his cheek, "You're not going to believe this, but they want me to tell you that if you go with the Belgians, the US government is no longer responsible for your safety. Also, you will need to sign off on their help. Basically, they want a record that you denied their offer."

I blinked at him. Was he serious?

"You mean to tell me that they sent you through those streets to give us...paperwork?"

"That's about right," he said.

I was too stunned to laugh.

"Really?" I finally blurted out. "And they sent you—*a Canadian*—to do it?"

"Oh, believe me," he said, "I've been puzzling over the same thing the entire way over here."

I couldn't hold back a smirk. It was too ridiculous. Apparently, this crisis was not going to be allowed to proceed until all of the proper paperwork had been properly signed!

I led him over to the other expats with whom I had been staying for the previous twenty-four hours and let him explain to them what he was doing there. After getting a similar reaction from the others in the group, we took turns signing the waiver, figuring that it was the least we could do for the poor guy who had just drove through the middle of a war zone from the American Club. When he was done, he thanked us, and left the way he came. We watched him disappear out through the entrance gate and on down the road.

We stood there, watching after him for some time. Seeing him successful at his trip made us again wonder aloud about the Muellers, where were they? How could we reach them? How would they get out if we were not able to get to them? I should just go get them. My mind returned many times to this idea, and I found myself staring at the truck, thinking through the route I would take.

I was in the middle of one such reverie when the air was suddenly filled with close range gunfire. All of us outside the chapel jumped at once. The people in the yard, too, began to flee in every direction. Hiding behind the doors of the chapel, we watched as little pellets hit the dirt and even the side of the chapel building. They were shooting at us, as well as into the crowded grassy area.

"Get down, get down!" People were yelling inside the chapel. Children began to cry as mothers and fathers dove for them and pulled them into a huddle within the walls. Just then, a shriek from the other side of the room caught all of our attention. We looked up to see one of the children—it was one of the young Pence boys—running through the door and out into the open.

"Get him! Stop him! Brian, come back here!" yelled his mother across the chapel.

Mimi, who was just inside the doorway, leapt to her feet and bolted out the front door after him. Several followed. As the young boy made a break for the grassy area at the side of the chapel, shrieking and giggling all the while, Mimi raced after him, bent forward at the waist. By the time she overtook him and tackled him to the ground, they were well off the side of the building. The boy, startled at being thrown to the ground, began to wail, crying at the injustice of having been treated so roughly when all he wanted to do was to play. Amidst the crackling gunfire, Mimi grabbed him around the chest and thighs and rushed him back to the chapel, where she immediately deposited him in Scott's arms.

"Thank you," he whispered, burying his nose in his son's neck. "Thank you."

"I was the closest," Mimi responded, quickly shrugging off any praise for what she had just done. "It's just where I was. God put me there. I didn't have anything to do with it."

TENSIONS RISING

JUNE 1993
KIGALI, RWANDA

"You must not stop stirring," said Agata, her eyes, yellowed and cloudy from too many years in the sun, remained steady on the pot. In one hand she held a fistful of white powder, which she sprinkled slowly into the boiling water, releasing a sour smell into the air. Her other hand swirled a wooden spoon around and around in the bubbling white porridge.

"You should stir the meat and the crushed leaves," she told Melanie, speaking only in Kinyarwanda, "It is time to add the peanut butter."

Melanie did as she was told, dutifully scooping up several large thick spoonfuls and dropping them into the bubbling green meat sauce. Agata continued at her post in front of the ugali, creating the thick porridge from manioc flour and water. More bush woman than city woman, Agata is a solid 5'4" wearing a bright blue and orange wrap on her head that matched the wraparound skirt that hung to her ankles. Aside from the seriousness with which she approaches matters of the kitchen, she is a jovial woman with a predisposition to express her opinion where she feels strongly. Alexi, her husband and my responsibility in mentorship, was by then a full-fledged pastor of his own church in Kigali. Together, we sat at the kitchen table and talked while the women worked at the stove. Outside, their seven children played with a ball in the yard on our compound.

We had been back in Rwanda for a couple of years since our wedding in Minnesota with our family and friends. Since our return, Melanie had been trying to learn how to adapt her cooking to better fit the availability of the various foods in Rwanda. And if there is one available food in Rwanda, it is manioc.

When I first moved to Rwanda, I had noticed the huge manioc—or cassava—tubers at the market and could not even imagine what one did with them. Some people roasted them wrapped in plantain leaves and sold them there at the market, but that was a huge leap from me buying one and attempting to cook it up at home. I had been informed that manioc is considered the world's third most common carbohydrate and that it contains large amounts of calcium and vitamin C in addition to the starch with which it is filled. The leaves are an excellent source of protein, even though they lack certain amino acids that would make the plant a complete food in and of itself. In the same conversation, however, I had also been warned that the tubers are filled with cyanide and would render a person paralyzed or even dead if prepared wrong. Needless to say, I had not felt overly compelled to cozy up to the plant. But Melanie, being the newlywed she was, had determined that she was committed to living in Africa and was going to learn to cook like an African. Thus, she needed a teacher, someone to show her the ropes and to keep her from, well, killing the two of us with her cooking.

"Perfect," said Agata to her eager student. "now, the onion and the palm oil."

"Is this right?" Asked Melanie, pointing to the onion she had chopped on a board next to the stove.

"Perfect," repeated Agata. Even as she said this, she made her way to the onions and in the blink of an eye expertly chopped them to a fraction of the size Melanie had managed earlier.

She paused to glance sideways at Melanie. "Do you have a lid?"

Dutifully, Melanie pulled one out from a shelf near the stove and held it out to her. Agata took the lid and trapped in the hot steam so that the ugali could further solidify and stay warm until we were ready to eat.

Fascinated, I watched the two of them working together. For me, African style cooking seems akin to magic, and I was impressed that Melanie had taken on the task with such resolve. Across from me at the kitchen table, Alexi was asking me about the Bible school back at Cyimbili. He had attended there while I was just a short-termer and was eager for news about some of the upcoming graduates.

"Hakizimana M. is finishing this year, as well as Alphonse S. There are several others. It is good to see such a bright class going out into the field," I told him.

At the stove, Agata dropped several long red chiles into the sauce. Melanie glanced at me to see if I had noticed. She bit back a grin when we made eye contact. The sauce was going to be spicy.

Beside me, Alexi shifted. I had known him long enough at that point to know that he had something to say on the matter.

"What is it?" I asked. "Do you know these men?"

He looked down at the table very seriously, adjusting a cup of tea that had gone cold on the table. Melanie caught the gesture and rushed to refill it from the teapot. Alexi nodded in gratitude.

"Alphonse," he said quietly. "To be honest, I do not trust him."

I looked at him, surprised. The man we were talking about had proven himself at the college. He was well respected amongst the current administration.

"I don't understand," I said. "He seems to be doing quite well. He has shown himself to be a godly man and has a charismatic personality that will serve him well as a pastor."

Alexi shook his head.

"It is true, he has a strong personality, but he is not as he seems. I have known him a long time."

"Perhaps he has changed since you knew him?" I asked. Agata turned from the stove to glance at her husband.

"He is from Agata's village," he said. "We know how he is."

"He will tell you one thing and do the other," said Agata from the stove. "He is a thief. This I know."

"He owes much money to many people," explained Alexi. "And there are rumors of his behavior with the women."

I was floored.

"Recently?"

Alexi nodded somberly and held his hands open.

"I am sorry to say, but I am telling you the truth, friend. The man is a fraud."

I leaned back in my seat, deeply troubled by what he was telling me. I will admit that I did not want to believe him. I liked Alphonse. Everyone liked Alphonse. How was it possible that we were all so far off on our assessment of him?

And yet, I knew that I could trust Alexi. Over the years we had known each other, he had proven himself time and again. Once when I had been in a meeting with several pastors from the area, I had grown upset over an issue we were discussing and showed my frustration. Afterwards, Alexi took me aside ever so gently, and explained to me that showing one's temper is perhaps not the best way to get what one wants in Rwanda. Emotion is something a person does not show in public—and especially agitation. It had not been easy for him to have to tell me that, but his candidness went a long ways with me. Over time, he had offered invaluable advice to me on matters too numerous to count. I knew I could trust him as a brother.

"Thank you," I told him, assuring him that I would watch Alphonse closely. While it was hard to believe that the wool had been pulled over my eyes so completely, I knew that I had to look into what Alexi was telling me. "It is good to have a trusted friend," I told him.

"These are difficult times," said Alexi.

I nodded, understanding full well what he meant. Since the invasion of the RPF Army on the night that Melanie and I were first scheduled for Indian food, things had gone from bad to worse in the Rwandan capital. While the government attempted to create and maintain treaties with the RPF, groups of Hutu-led citizens stirred up unrest. Rumors of Tutsis being taken in the night began to circulate. Days later, variations on these rumors would surface, causing everyone to wonder if anything they ever heard was real.

Meanwhile, gunfire and explosions in the city were becoming a common background noise. On one occasion, when the RPF representatives came to the Rwandan Parliament building to discuss a peace treaty, a battalion of nearly 500 RPF soldiers came to accompany them, filling the city with their presence. As a result, the Interahamwe mobs stepped up their own actions, ambushing other local groups who supported the treaty. When our friend, Tim Okken, was shot in the hand, it was an ambush like this that he had inadvertently crossed into.

We all knew the story. Tim and his father were driving back from an errand at the airport. As they were driving down the street, they spotted a group of men with guns. Thinking that their friends behind them needed to be warned, they stopped the car and began to turn around. And that's when things fell apart.

When the first shots were fired, Tim put pedal to metal trying to get the car facing the other direction. Bullets ripped through the car doors and windows as he stripped the gears and the car lurched forward and away from the men with guns. But despite his best efforts, six bullets entered the cab of the vehicle, one sinking into his father's leg and another barely missing his knee only to rocket straight through the hand that was on the stick shift through the joint of his right thumb. Three others barely missed his head through the driver's side door.

There were other signs of unrest leading up to the genocide in 1994. Throughout the years after the RPF invasion in 1990 leading up to the genocide, we could look across the valley and see the main road, and hear the people chanting. Once in the morning after one of these gatherings, I came upon a man who had been badly beaten in the night and lay breathing his last strained breaths at the street's edge. But these uprisings would come, and then they would go. The embassy would call us once a month to tell us not to go out. And then, the situation would improve, and we could move freely around the city.

"Things will get better," we would tell ourselves, believing that the way you stayed safe was to keep your head down and to not go out after dark.

These times came in surges. Rumors would circulate that the Hutu militia were plotting something big against the Tutsis. On the radio, people would stir up dissention against the Tutsi people, making up rumors and telling the Hutu militia members to wait for a sign when they should attack. "You will know when it is time," they were told from the airwaves.

It would be so bad in the city for a while that we would not dare go out after dark, and then it would be almost normal again. There was nothing we could do but watch and wait.

"Do you think it's wise for us to stay here?" I asked Melanie once when stories of violence were escalating. So much had been happening around us that many of our friends and family back home were beginning to openly question whether it was safe for us to stay. We had received more than one heartfelt letter from home, begging us to reconsider our direction.

As far back as our wedding there had been people questioning the wisdom of remaining in Rwanda. My brother Randy asked pointed questions about how safe it was. In one of our conversations he said, "Don't be a martyr unless you absolutely have to!" I laughed and replied, "I don't plan on being one!"

While I knew that my heart was in Rwanda, I was concerned about Melanie. I wanted to know what she felt God was leading us to do. Together, we prayed, seeking direction from the Lord. Should we take what had happened to Tim Okken as a sign that it was time to head home, or should we stay there, trusting in God to lead our footsteps? When we were done praying, I looked up at Melanie. I will never forget her face in that moment.

"Our Rwandan friends don't have a choice," she said quietly.

And even as she said it, I knew. We needed to stay there. We needed to walk beside them, our Rwandan friends who did not have a choice and could not escape to a safer country. And no, we were under no illusion that God would necessarily choose to keep us safe. I had cast off that impression many years before. Had not E.J. Kile been a godly man? Had not many others who had been called home in their prime? Too many times have I seen good, godly people suffer. But I hold strong to the belief that nothing happens in life without God's permission. God would be with us no matter what, be it in life or in death. If we were going to be hurt or even die in Rwanda, then so be it. Our place was there.

As I watched Melanie and Agata in the kitchen while Alexi and I talked that day, the sour smell of the ugali mixing with the deeper aroma of the meat sauce and permeating each one of us to our core, I knew we had made the right decision to stay. Whatever happened to us, our lives were intertwined with Rwanda and its people.

Whatever happened, we could not just leave.

THE LEGIONNAIRES

APRIL 11, 1994
KIGALI, RWANDA

We slept through the second night in shifts. We did not plan it that way, it just happened. We could hear the men's voices carrying through the night as they discussed position and strategy out on the street. Every now and then somebody would shout and we would brace ourselves for what might happen next, although it rarely happened that way. A yell was no less a cue for incoming fire than a sneeze would be for the call to be evacuated. There was no logic. Nothing made sense. Nothing was predictable. When the gunfire started, it was frequently without warning. It happened suddenly and was all-consuming. We would awaken and reach for each other in the dark. When it was over, one of us would go back to sleep, the other would listen. By the time the other fell asleep, the other would waken. I listened to Melanie breathe in her sleep for hours.

When Monday morning came, we rose stiffly and one by one, went outside. Nothing visibly had changed. The Rwandans stood in the yard, speaking quietly. Friends comforted friends, husbands and wives comforted each other and their children, mothers held infants to their backs. The UN soldiers continued to stand guard, stationed strategically at certain buildings. We were given breakfast rations. The cargo planes droned overhead, an ever-present reminder that we might be called upon to leave at any time.

Throughout it all, we expected the arrival of reinforcements at any time. We had been told repeatedly by the UN soldiers that more troops were on the way. It was only a matter of time before the international community would join in to help. There was no way that blatant genocide would be allowed to continue, right?

And then, as if in answer to prayer, the French Foreign Legion stormed in. They drove confiscated vehicles, were dressed in camouflaged body armor and were armed with FAMAS rifles, as well as a variety of other combat accoutrements. The sight of them was like manna from heaven. *Finally*, we thought. *Finally!*

They drove straight onto the compound and exchanged words with the Belgian UN soldiers. It was 10:00 a.m.

"We are here to evacuate your expats," said the Legionnaires in French.

"We have it under control," effectively answered the Belgians, to which the Legionnaires responded by pointing out the cargo planes uselessly circling overhead.

"We are here to evacuate your expats," repeated the Legionnaires.

The entire argument lasted less than twenty minutes. According to the French Foreign Legion, they had secured part of the airport and were taking over the evacuation. Finally, the Belgians had to concede. Having thus won the argument, the Legionnaires instructed us to line up our vehicles, strategically interspersed with what they called "military vehicles," in other words, civilian vehicles they had confiscated and off of which they had ripped the doors. Phil and I hesitated.

"We can't leave without the Muellers," said Phil, pulling me aside.

"I agree. I don't feel like we've done everything we can do," I answered.

"But if we drive out to their house, it could be bad," he pointed out. "I can't believe we can't get a UN soldier to accompany us."

He was shaking his head with frustration and shifting agitatedly. Mimi approached us from the side.

"Honey?"

Phil softened slightly.

"I just don't feel right about this."

Mimi placed her hand on his shoulder.

"None of us do. What's there to feel right about?"

Melanie came up to us as well and stood at my side.

"Are you ready?" she asked. "The soldiers want us out of here." She looked around at our faces. "It's the Muellers, isn't it?"

We nodded.

As we spoke, a Tutsi man dressed in a business suit and who was well connected within the former government approached us. I recognized him.

"Please, you must take me with you," he said to me.

I didn't know what to say. I wanted to assist him, but I felt helpless in the face of what the soldiers had told us.

"They aren't allowing nationals," I sputtered out, not sure what I could do.

"We'll take you," said a voice beside me. It was Larry Randolph. "Get in the car."

He did and Larry started his engine. He pulled slowly into position in the line-up. When nobody stopped them, I felt sad that I had denied him. I felt thick, as if my brain were not working quite right. When a couple from Ghana with whom we had been with in the chapel for the previous two days asked if they could ride with us to the airport, I said yes right away.

Just then one of the Legionnaires approached us.

"It's time to move, people. You see those vehicles?" He asked, pointing at more than twenty cars lining up at the gate. "We need to join them...Now!"

Phil and I exchanged glances.

"We have friends that are still out there," he told the soldier in fluent French. Phil has always had a gift for languages.

"I'm sorry to hear that, sir. My orders, however, are to accompany you to the airport."

"I understand. But if the opportunity presents itself, I would like to go with you to their house," said Phil.

The soldier sniffed a laugh.

"That would be highly unlikely," he said. "Let's go."

The Bjorklunds went to their vehicle and got in with them while Melanie and I piled into the car with the Ghanaian couple. We lined up to leave.

As we did this, we noticed that the Tutsi people around us were getting nervous.

"Where are you going?" shouted a few of them from the fenced area.

"Don't abandon us—take me with you!" yelled another. "Don't leave!"

Don't leave. The words echoed through my head like a conviction. How could we be leaving?

I looked over at Melanie, torn between my former resolution to stay no matter what happened and knowing that if we stayed we would likely be killed.

Wishing desperately that we could do something, we also knew that there was nothing we could actually do. Beside me in the cab, Melanie breathed deeply as she, too, wrestled with the reality of the situation.

The convoy lurched forward and we pulled away. As we left the gate, Melanie looked back at the people calling out to us on the green behind us.

"They're going to protect them and put an end to this, right?"

"Yes," I answered, overcome with the realization that the people in that yard needed more help than what we could offer. How could we help? How could we even stand by them? The situation had changed. I had a different responsibility now. I had to help get Melanie and my friends to safety. The danger was so far beyond what I thought we might face. It was no longer a possibility, but a certainty. The Belgian soldiers were still there to protect the Tutsis that had gathered. More troops had been called in. They would put an end to the terror. I believed that. I *had* to believe that. And now, I had to get Melanie out of there. I felt it in the marrow of my bones.

"Please God," I prayed silently, "protect those people. Please keep them safe."

We followed the convoy down a back way by a swamp. We felt drained. Numb to emotion. Our hearts were back with the crowd we had left behind. As we approached populated areas, we passed hundreds of people wandering the streets. I have never put much stock in tales of zombies, but looking out over the streets of Kigali on that day, it was not difficult to imagine the truth in such stories. Each person wore the same glazed over look and carried a weapon in his or her hand. Some had sticks, others had knives. Most walked around aimlessly as if they had no real sense of where they were or where they should be. Only that they were there to kill. They, themselves, hardly seemed alive.

Several times, we turned off the road we were on and onto another in order to avoid these mobs. When we realized that we were somewhat lost, we cut across a cow pasture. The truck jerked and jostled as we drove over the bumpy ground.

"I hope everyone's got a seatbelt on," I said from behind the wheel, my head jostling on my neck.

Melanie gripped the strap over her chest and glanced back at our passengers seated behind us. The woman, dressed in a rich, purple cloth, gazed kindly back at her from beside her husband as she did so.

"We are OK," she said. "Please, do not worry over us."

Melanie nodded back, an indication of her gratitude for their graciousness in the midst of our circumstances.

Ahead of us, the Scheers' vehicle bounced over a rut in the pasture and we watched as the passengers shot upwards slightly in their seats. Just then, the spare tire attached to the back of their truck came dislodged and fell off, bouncing away over the damp earth. I pulled to a stop and flung my door wide in order to chase after it, rolling, rolling, rolling in the opposite direction. Finally, it settled on its side and I pounced on it and jogged it back to where the Scheers had stopped their truck. Gary hopped out of his car and together we secured it back in place.

"Unbelievable," he said, scratching his head and smiling awkwardly.

"Never saw that coming," I agreed.

I got back in the car and pressed on the gas to catch up to the convoy on up ahead of us. Just as we started to roll, we heard a loud voice from outside the car. We turned to look to see a man, dressed in a blue shirt and brown pants. He wore flip-flops on his feet. In each of his hands, he wielded a *mpanga*.

"They are getting away with Tutsi cockroaches! Stop them!" He yelled, chasing after us slicing the air at the Ghanaian couple in our truck.

"Dear God," began Melanie as we bulleted forward. It was then that I noticed that we were nearing another pile of bodies—close to thirty this time.

"Don't look," I blurted out as quickly as I could. I thought about the others in the convoy, the children. Before we had left, I overheard the Scheers telling their children, "If we say close your eyes, CLOSE your eyes!" I could only hope the children were doing as they were told.

Behind us, the man continued to run after us. In my rearview mirror, I watched as he chased us as far as he could go before we were out of sight.

Forced to take a side road into the airport, we cut through a neighborhood filled with small houses. Immediately, we realized our mistake. The route was almost entirely blocked. Bodies, disfigured and crumpled, lay lifeless in the street where they had been cut down, men, women, and children. So many children... Blood pooled thick like mud in the road. There was no way through unless we drove off the road, up into people's yards. The entire convoy had slowed to a crawl. None of us spoke—none of us could speak. There was nothing to say. Even the air around us was stilled to a hush in this graveyard, this open tomb. We wound our way as best we could, maneuvering past limbs and occasionally forced to move over them when there was no other possible way.

I'm sorry, I said in my head as we passed. *I'm so, so sorry.*

The anger I had felt back at Don Bosco had returned with a vengeance. Where was the international community? Where were the soldiers fighting back the evil that was happening all over this land? I thought about the French Legionnaires who had come to chaperone us out. Were there more like them on the way?

And with this anger came a new emotion...guilt. How could I leave? How could I abandon our friends? Rwanda and I were intertwined. Leaving felt like a betrayal, even as we drove past the bodies of those whom we could never have saved, let alone stood beside.

I don't remember the rest of the route to the airport. It is a blank in my mind. All I know is that we arrived and we parked.

Before long, one of the Legionnaires approached my window.

"Sorry, Americans. The Belgian paratroopers have just arrived. Our first priority is to get out the Belgians."

"What?" We asked incredulously. "Are you telling us that we can't get on a plane?"

"We shall see about that. For now, please leave your keys in your vehicles."

Looking closely at him, I realized that what he was telling us was that they were planning to take our cars from us. I stared at him as if through the eyes of a ghost. Were it not for Melanie beside me, I would not have had anything left.

"No, thanks," I said. "I'd like to keep my keys with me."

He looked me in the eye for a moment before looking away, a slight curl to the edge of his mouth.

"If you do not leave your keys, then we will just break the windows and hotwire the vehicle anyway."

I left the keys.

We followed him across the runway to a hangar where we registered our names on yet another list and placed in line for the next available plane. The place was filled with others—mostly Belgians—also trying to get out. We were told that the plane was on a delayed departure.

Soon after, we spotted a convoy of military vehicles headed down the road toward us. It did not take us long to recognize them. They were the Belgian soldiers we had left back at Don Bosco. It had been about an hour since our departure.

"What? Why are they…?" began Melanie before fading off.

We watched them from the entrance to the hangar, horrified. If they were here, who was protecting the people back at the school?

They pulled into the lot and parked nearby, bursting out of the cars the minute they rolled to a stop. Several of the soldiers went storming off in opposite directions, as if trying to compose themselves through their anger, their jaws set and eyes low. Many of them threw their blue berets on the ground.

"What are you doing here?" I asked the first one I could get close to. "Who is protecting the people at Don Bosco?"

The soldier to whom I had posed the question stopped in his tracks. He spoke to me without looking at me.

"Nobody is protecting them. We were ordered out. As we drove away, the Interahamwe poured in. People were throwing themselves in front of our cars." He paused, audibly choking down a lump in his throat. "There will be no one left."

I watched him in shock as he marched away.

"No," said Melanie, who had joined me at my side. She had overheard what the soldier had said. I took her in my arms and held her tightly as she wept… There were no words.

How could the soldiers have left? Who would have made such an order? I wanted to yell at somebody. The soldiers. The captain. Who had given that order?

As news trickled to the other members of our small group, we could hear strained sobs from all around us. Several people came up and put their arms around us. But there was no comfort, only shock and anger.

"I would never have agreed to leave if I thought that it would put those people at risk," said Melanie when she could speak again. And that's when it hit me. I was feeling more than shock and anger or even guilt. I was feeling a deep sense of shame.

Just then, Phil jogged up to where we were standing.

"I'll be back," he said, determination in his voice.

"What?" Asked Mimi, her voice catching. "Where are you going?"

"To check the Muellers' house," he said. "The soldiers said I could go with them."

"Yes," I whispered. Something inside of me stirred. Melanie shot me a look. I was still in trouble for leaving her back at Don Bosco. This I knew. And still, it was something to hold onto. It was small, but it was there, a glimmer of hope.

"Why don't you just let the soldiers go?" Mimi asked Phil, still visibly pale and shaking from the drive over.

"They don't know the area and I want to make sure this gets done," answered Phil. He did not need to remind us about the people of Don Bosco. There were no guarantees anyone would be safe. If he didn't check on the Muellers, who would? After what had happened, we could not allow anything to be taken for granted. "I'll be safe with the soldiers."

He hugged a now speechless Mimi. When he was done, he paused to make eye contact with me.

"You stay here and protect them," he said, understanding at once by my expression how desperately I wanted to accompany him and, at the same time, how much I needed to stay with Melanie. But his statement was direct and it gave me a sense of dignity in my duty, regardless of how much I knew it had been uttered entirely for that purpose.

I nodded and reached out my hand to him. He took it, grasping it firmly for a couple seconds. And then he took his leave.

"God will protect him," said Mimi then, turning to Laurie and Melanie. "I have to believe it."

Even as she said it, her eyes welled up slightly.

"He's doing the right thing," the women assured her. All of us were poignantly aware of the Muellers' absence.

We found a place at the side of the hangar to settle the children. Few of us spoke about what we had seen. The faces of our friends said it all. The Tutsi wives of the Belgians amongst us wept openly. There was no consoling them. Together, we found what corners we could in the space and sat there—some of us alone, others in groups—but all of us there, present though we desperately wished to be elsewhere.

Outside the hangar, we watched the Belgians load the large C-130 Hercules cargo plane up the back ramp with their luggage. Several of them bore large suitcases, not constrained by size or weight like we had been. A few of them even had their dogs with them.

When it was just past 4:30, one of the Belgian paratroopers approached our group to let us know that there was still some room left on the plane. This would have been great news except for the fact that Phil had not yet returned from his last attempt to find news about the Muellers.

"We can't leave," I said to one of the soldiers over the roar of the engines. "We have a man out with the French troops."

He shook his head at me.

"I'm sorry to hear that, sir. He had better hurry. We can't wait."

"I'm not leaving without him or the Muellers," I said, suddenly uncertain of my own conviction. Melanie looked sternly at me.

"Sir, it would seem you don't have much of a choice. My orders are to get you on that plane."

We lined up behind the plane. Mimi was clearly nervous. The soldiers were making final preparations to leave.

"I can't leave without him," she said, knowing as she said it that she had to get her children on the plane. "How can I?" Her oldest daughter held her around the waist and sobbed into her arm.

Slowly, we moved forward in the line toward the ramp. Phil had been gone for more than an hour now. There was not a one of us who was not staring out toward the road. More agonizing suspense, would he make it? Would we be forced to leave without him?

Just as they were about to usher us up the back ramp, a vehicle sped across the tarmac. The door opened wide and a person got out. It was Phil!

Relief swept over everybody as Phil took his place by Mimi and their kids.

"Thank you, Lord," whispered Mimi into Phil's neck.

Just then, somebody ran up to us and relayed the news we had been waiting for.

"They got out! They got out!" he said. "The Muellers left on the very first flight yesterday!"

We erupted in a cheer. It was what we had been waiting for. Several of us teared up with the news.

We took our places on the floor of the plane. There is no separate passenger compartment on a C-130, so we sat facing each other in columns lengthwise across the plane. Soon after we were settled, the huge four engines of the turbo prop roared as we prepared to take off and the back ramp was closed. The power of the plane vibrated through our feet on the cool metal floor. We were airborne within minutes, flying low to the ground to avoid being shot at.

Standing to look out one of the small, round windows that intermittently lined the walls, I could see at a glance the mass destruction of the city. Everywhere I looked I saw buildings destroyed and groups of people in the streets. Fires burned openly in several areas and smoke rose to the sky, meeting the clouds in columns.

Making my way carefully back to my place, I sat down hard. I was exhausted. Melanie, beside me, gripped my hand tightly. I looked over at her to see that she had pressed her eyelids together. She was holding her breath, too overcome with emotion to speak.

Several feet down from us, Larry Randolph stood from his place next to his wife Diane and walked over to the window where I had been moments before. He watched silently out the window for several minutes. Without warning, he covered his face with his hands, consumed in grief.

He began sobbing, loud enough for us to hear over the roar of the engines, he said, "The Rwanda we knew is gone forever."

Melanie and I sat huddled together, our fingers intertwined as tears slipped down our faces. As far as we were concerned, we had made a commitment to stay there to stand by and support our friends. As it turned out, it was a commitment we would not be able to keep. Our hearts, like our home, had been shattered.

STATIC

APRIL - JUNE 1994
WINDOM, MN

For the next three months we watched helplessly through a televised lens as evil leveled Rwanda down to its foundation. While the United Nations bickered over the terminology of genocide, men turned on their neighbors—seeking them out in churches and basements, pulling them out from underneath their mattresses—and put them to death. When it was all over, more than 800,000 had fallen, mostly by the machete or by spiked club. It did not matter if they were man, woman or child. If they were Tutsi, they were labeled "cockroach," and then brutally and relentlessly killed.

We were on the move for two weeks after our evacuation: first in Nairobi, then to Mombasa, then back to Nairobi, before finally heading home. Of course home is a somewhat misleading term. Melanie and I had no home in the US. There were the places we had each grown up, but there was no house in a place we called ours. After we had been married, we had returned to Rwanda. That was where our home was. And now, we were not sure if we even had a home at all. It seemed everything we thought we knew had changed.

We were consumed by the unknown. We did not know if our Rwandan friends were alive or whether they lay somewhere pressed together in a mass grave. It did not matter if they were Hutu or Tutsi. Our Hutu friends were considered "moderates" and would have been viewed just the same as the Tutsis they would have sought to help. Had they been discovered, theirs would also have been an immediate sentence to death.

We feared for Anastaz, the Tutsi pastor of our church. We feared for Rosa and her family who last we heard lived in the city of Ruengheri, for Alexi and Agata and their now eight children. Melanie's heart broke for the children she had helped tutor and care for in the neighborhood. We remembered her Tutsi language teacher, Christine whom we had once had to rescue from the local group of Interahamwe as she walked to the taxi stand after teaching Melanie one day. We were concerned for the many Tutsi families in our church who we had come to know and love over the years of spending time and worshipping with them. Across the country, I had developed relationships with so many beautiful people, both Tutsi and Hutu, who loved the Lord deeply and who would never be a part of such evil.

As we watched and waited for news—*any news*—of our Rwandese friends, the numbness of my initial shock began to wear off. I began to feel outrage and, I am sorry to say, anger to my very core. I could feel it inside of me, hot like fire and bitter around the edges. I had dedicated my life to the Lord's work in that country, and now I was forced to sit back and watch it slip away. I thought about my years on the coffee plantation with the Kiles and Rosa and the people at the Bible School. I thought about traveling the country with the Jesus Film. I thought about the churches I had helped build and the many roofs I had constructed. I thought about all of the beautiful people in the church I had met and who had blessed me with their gentle spirits. What had happened to them? Were they dead? Were they alive? And what would become of the churches we had built? What would become of any of it? Had everything we had worked for shattered and fallen? Did anything we had worked so hard to build have any meaning at all?

The genocide lasted for one hundred days. For one hundred days I prayed for peace and for the protection of our friends.

Lord, please bring peace to the people of Rwanda.

Please protect our friends.

Please protect our ministry in Your name.

Please help me push past this anger so that I can again be useful to You.

When it was all over and the numbers were in and there was nothing more to do, I could only sit still in the unknown and wait. I waited and waited on the Lord until the walls seemed to press inward and my head felt thick, as if the air was filled with static.

Please, I continued to pray over and again, *Hear our prayers, oh Lord.*

GOING BACK

JULY 1994
WHEATON, IL – UGANDA/CONGO

Melanie and I made the decision to go back together. I don't remember being nervous; we wanted to do it. Despite the objections of several well-meaning friends and family we felt compelled to go.

Besides, there was nobody else who could logically go. The Scheers had kids and were scheduled to be home. The Bjorklunds, too, had kids. Tim Okken was recovering from surgery on his hand. The Muellers not only had kids, they had not really even had a chance to learn the language yet.

Back at headquarters in Wheaton, IL, we looked across the boardroom table at the president of our mission board. It was nearing the end of July. Kigali had fallen only two weeks before.

"We'll go," I said.

"Are you sure that both of you are OK with the risks involved?" he asked. "I don't have to tell you that the Rwanda you are returning to is not going to be anything like the Rwanda you left."

Melanie glanced at me and nodded. We remembered all too well the words of our friend Larry Randolph as we flew out of Kigali. *The Rwanda we knew is gone forever.* But we could not stay away, either. Our place was in Rwanda. Our *home* was in Rwanda. There was nothing we wanted more than to go back, find our Rwandese colleagues and friends who had survived, and help them pick up the pieces. Even if we could help only a little bit, it was what we urgently wanted to do.

"We understand the risks," we said. And we meant it. Even so, we had no idea what we would be returning to.

Since the airport in Kigali was not functional, we flew in to Kampala, Uganda. We had a team of missionaries up there already and there was an apartment where we could stay. It would be our base station. Now, all we needed was to figure out how to get around. We already knew that my truck was long gone. We took it to God in prayer. It did not take long for him to answer.

When the killing had begun, Tudy Kile had fled to Goma, Congo (DRC) in her yellow 1984 Toyota Corolla. Having returned back to the States, she left the vehicle in the care of another mission organization. After a couple of telephone conversations, we learned that the car was currently about a four-hour bus ride from where we were stationed. We took the bus from Uganda into the Democratic Republic of Congo, found the car, and then drove the rest of the way towards the refugee camps. We were in an area where several refugee camps were located. Since our mission had a hospital there and we wanted to be close to these camps, would set up a second base here.

We had made it about thirty kilometers north of Goma when we caught our first glimpse of one of the refugee camps. It being the rainy season, the skies were gray and the air was filled with moisture. We were on the tar road and had just crested a hill when we saw it—a massive sea of white, green and blue tents.

Hardly able to process the size of it, I slowed the car down so that we could get a better look. Not thousands, but tens of thousands of tents, stretched as far as the eye could see off into the horizon and beyond. And with the sight, the weight of what had happened once again crushed sideways and on top of us. So much so that I had to pull off to the side of the road.

We stared for nearly a minute without saying anything to one another. Until that moment, we had only heard about the massive human exodus that had taken place. We had seen clips on television of the conditions of the camps and seen shots taken in newspapers. But this...this was real and it was directly in front of us.

"How could this happen?" I heard Melanie ask at a whisper beside me. "I still can't..." She stopped.

I could only shake my head. It was bigger than us, the two of us there. We had come back to try and help where we could. To find the people we knew and help them put their lives back together. To try and piece back together the work we had labored so hard to put into place.

Looking over that refugee camp through the windshield of Tudy's Corolla that day, I realized that the task was so much bigger than I had even imagined. It would be slow and painful. There would be difficulties and angles I could not conceive of in that moment. It was going to be like moving an ocean, one bucket at a time, back to where it belonged.

Never before had I felt so small.

SEARCHING

AUGUST 1994
NEAR GOMA, CONGO (DRC)

What seemed like an impossible search, slowly began to resolve itself. Little by little we made contact with our people. In Rwanguba our mission had a Bible School with extra housing, and—miraculously—a number of our people had managed to make their way there. Even more incredible, it was here that one of my biggest prayers was answered. It was here that we found Alexi.

"Brother," he said as he approached. He had been told that we would be coming soon. When he saw the yellow car pull up, he came out to see who it was.

Blinking at him in disbelief, I held my hand out to him. His face was somewhat gaunt, but his eyes were as alive as they had ever been. Even so, there was a sadness that lined him like a cloud.

"I don't believe it," I said. "How in the world did you survive?"

He shook his head as if he did not quite understand it himself.

"Only by the grace of God alone."

"Agata and your children—are they with you?"

He nodded.

"When did you get out?" I asked, still overwhelmed by having found him.

"We stayed until the first of July," he explained. "The fighting was so bad, so heavy. That first day, we left early in the morning and walked fifty kilometers to Gitarama. As we walked, bullets and mortars flew all around us. People were killed right in front of us. We are lucky to be alive. We walked for many days until we made it here. Praise God, I still have my family.... So many of us...do not."

I looked at him closely then. Here was a man who had seen so much pain and suffering. And yet, he stood before me able to praise God for what he still had. I fought back my emotions, trying desperately to respect his Rwandan need for that distance.

SHREDDED PIECES

JULY 1994
KIGALI, RWANDA

On the day of our return to Kigali, the city was still pretty much deserted. Everywhere, buildings lay wasted and in ruin. There were no markets. No restaurants. No place to even buy fuel. Only a few people walked the streets. Nobody sat in windows. The place felt empty like a tomb.

As we turned off the main tar road into our neighborhood, we barely recognized our surroundings. Houses that we had considered landmarks had been turned into piles of rubble. Others were missing windows, walls or parts of their roofs.

A few blocks from our house we came upon the burned out remains of a minivan, partially blocking the road. As we neared it, we could see that it had hit a land mine buried in the road, leaving a gaping hole in the middle of it and all of the windows blown out into the street. The passengers of the minivan had been torn to pieces in the blast, the clothes that they had been wearing the only testament left to their former presence. Bright, multi-colored pieces of fabric lay wedged between mud, steel and bone, fluttering gently in the wind. From that point on, we were careful to drive in the tracks made by other vehicles, meticulously avoiding untested ground.

As we approached our yellow metal gate, we strained to see what we could of our house and were quite preoccupied with the task when we suddenly realized that we were being chased.

"Stop the car," said Melanie, excitedly.

I stopped and she opened the car door. Before I even knew what had happened, she was being enveloped in hugs by three small children.

"Melania! Melania!" they cried, chanting her name, dancing and clapping their hands. Tears streamed down her face as she reached out for them and held them tightly. I watched them all in their reunion, my own throat growing tight.

In front of us on the other side of the gate, I could see that our house had been hit hard.

Beside me, the children talked excitedly to Melanie and asked her if she had come back to stay. She explained to them that we would be back and forth while we repaired the house but that she would get to see them now and then and maybe even color with them again soon.

With that promise in hand, the children headed back down the street to their homes and we turned our attention toward our house. Unable to get through the gate, we walked around and through a gaping hole in what had once been the eight-foot-high wall surrounding the compound. Before us, we had the first clear glimpse of our house and could scarcely comprehend what we saw.

To begin, we could see that the roof was nearly one-third missing. Walking around the house, we discovered a large patch of blood that was not very old. Later we would piece together that there had been a land mine and a soldier had stepped on it just a few days prior to our getting there. In tandem with the minivan we had passed on the way there, our first lesson in the new Rwanda was clear: we could take nothing for granted. Not food, not water...not even the ground in front of us.

Entering the house through a wide-open door, we quickly discovered that the ceilings were all gone, as were all of the windows. Most of the household items and furniture were totally gone as well, having either been looted or destroyed. The home did not belong to us. Even so, seeing it like that felt like a kick to the gut.

I had first noticed the fabric out in the yard. I saw more pieces of it inside the house, shredded and blown to the corners of the rooms and draped across other piles of ruined objects. Although familiar, I could not place it at first. When I realized at long last what it was, something inside of me shifted.

It was the tent.

SHREDDED PIECES

The same one I had obsessed over during those first days when the Rwandan army had moved next door to us and had begun firing uphill toward the invading RPF army.

It rained that first night back, leading us to set up the newer tent we had brought with us in our living room because of the absent roof. It was the first time I ever camped inside of my own home! We woke up the next morning surrounded by a large puddle of water, amazed that we had managed to stay dry.

As I looked around at the rainwater-drenched room in the morning light, I caught sight again of one of the shredded pieces from the tent I had been so careful to bring in out of the rain and gunfire. It was soaked through and lay in a gnarled strip over a toppled end table. Before we had left the house on the day of our departure, I had taken that tent up to the attic in an attempt to keep it safe. I had not been able to protect it. I had not been able to protect any of it.

How is it that we had managed to stay dry?

SURVIVAL

JULY 1994
RWANDA / UGANDA / CONGO (DRC)

It was at this point that we began to live in a triangle. We traveled by vehicle to Uganda for supplies, over to Congo to visit the refugee camps and to help out at the hospital and then down to Kigali to rebuild our house. Over and over again, each week we did this.

During the weekends, we would set out for the camps. Alexi often accompanied us.

The camps—Katale, Kahindo, Mugunga. How can I convey in words what we saw there? With more than 2 million refugees displaced from Rwanda, each camp contained hundreds of thousands of people in close-knit quarters in makeshift tents made of white, green and blue tarps stamped with the letters UNHCR. Draped over whatever sticks people could find, these tents stood at about 4 x 5 meters and were haphazardly arranged by the refugees into "streets," littered with cooking pots, buckets and whatever else could possibly be found to aid in the daily functions of life. People of all ages and quality of health sat outside their tents, some with cloths draped over their heads to keep off the drizzle, and all wearing the very same clothes on their backs that they had walked out of Rwanda with months before. Many spoke with their neighbors and moved freely about the camps while others sat listlessly, watching without processing what was happening around them.

There was a little food, thanks to the relief efforts of more than 200 aid organizations from around the world. Rice and beans were distributed twice weekly. Firewood was collected where it could be found and kept close to the three-stone fireplaces people had constructed. The UN was trucking water in regularly and filling large canvas bladders where people could then collect it.

And there was disease. With no outhouses constructed at the beginning, people were at the mercy of the cramped conditions and close quarters. Human waste lay openly in the streets and around the edges of the camps. Only a month before our arrival, a large dysentery and cholera outbreak had moved through the camps, picking off the weak and the young. The dead were wrapped loosely with blankets and straw mats and stacked in long multiple rows along the road like firewood for the UN to collect. During this time, people died at the rate of 600 per week. Near the end of July, one twenty-four hour period saw the deaths of nearly 7,000 people at the camp in Goma, alone. Since the camp was located on a volcanic plain, the ground was so hard that UN workers were unable to dig graves for the deceased. Apprised of the situation half a world away, President Bill Clinton called the event, "The worst humanitarian crisis in a generation." When all was said and done, by August, more than 50,000 refugees had died, mostly due to cholera.

Many countries rallied to help the refugees. The US agreed to provide some aid, dropping large packages of food from above in hopes that it would help relieve hunger. Instead, mobs of people trying to get to the food ended up fighting each other. Many were killed.

Over the month, the situation was exacerbated even further by rain. As the cholera began to recede, others began to contract septic meningitis.

So many loved ones had been lost, if not by death, then in the chaos of the massive human migration that had taken place on foot. Families had been separated, with children in one camp and parents in another, neither knowing if the other was still alive. Few had the energy left to walk, let alone laugh. When disease swept through the camps, there was hardly anything left with which to fight. Exhausted, men, women and children sat limply in the openings of their tents.

Alexi took me around to those whom he knew in the camps and introduced me. There were several he had known through the church. He knew

SURVIVAL

the stories of so many families—those who had lost loved ones and those who did not know whether their families had lived or died.

When we left to head back to Kigali after our first visit to the Goma camp, he handed me a small list.

"These are the names of some people here. They believe that their families may have gotten lost and ended up in other camps. Please, keep watch for them."

We nodded in agreement before taking our leave.

"We will be back," we assured him, and headed back to Kigali.

CURTAINS

SEPTEMBER 1994
KIGALI, RWANDA

In Kigali, the work was intense, difficult, a constant struggle. Since there were no markets or stores operating, we had to bring all of the supplies we would need with us. There was no electricity, no running water, no phone service, and no gas for our vehicles. Each trip we made we came loaded down with food and water for the week, Jerry cans filled with gas, building materials, charcoal, and anything we could carry to help restock the house.

Anything of value or use in the house had been emptied. Clothes we had left behind were gone, as were blankets, curtains, cookware and utensils. Any medicines left in the bathroom cabinets had disappeared, as well as any remaining food or even paper. We had to start from scratch. And still, we knew we were lucky. Our friend Scott Pence had had to confront a family who was moving into his house upon his return and actively throwing his books out on the lawn.

Little by little, over time, we brought things back with us from the stores in Uganda. Plates and silverware, towels...whatever we needed in order to rebuild our lives there. During the day we would sometimes make a trek over to a place nicknamed the "Thieves Market" where people who had collected unclaimed items left behind in the mass exodus and loss of human life sold what they had found. Several times I discovered items of mine—still labeled with my name—and bought them back from people I had never met before.

It never really bothered me, having to buy back my own things. The people doing the selling were not likely the ones who had done the taking in the first place. Most of those people were long gone along with the criminals who had carried out the killings during the genocide; gone to the jungles and hidden areas of Congo and other surrounding countries. The little old woman or young man selling me back my own cooler or file box was simply trying to eke out a small existence the only way they could. Besides, I was usually too overjoyed to find anything that had once been mine to be upset. There were no other stores in which I could easily replace them.

One morning, soon after our return, a woman arrived at our gate with her arms filled with a pile of items.

"I saw that you were back," she told us, sheepishly, "and thought you might need these."

She held out to me her arms stuffed with fabric and various objects.

"Our dining room curtains!" I said excitedly, recognizing at once the large blue flowers on a pink background. Since the house was not ours and we could not paint it the colors we would have otherwise, the curtains had been a happy compromise to make the place feel like ours. They had been on our list of items to replace, of course, but so far we had not gotten around to doing it yet. Besides, it was likely that we would have to make the curtains ourselves and we did not exactly have a functional sewing machine in our possession at that point. Even if we did, it would have been somewhat useless with the lack of electricity. I reached out to help relieve her of her burden.

"Please," I told her, "come inside. My wife will be so happy to see these."

"I felt bad, but when I got back my house didn't have anything in it," she explained to Melanie once she made it up the driveway to the entrance. "Your house was there so I went in and…helped myself. I am very sorry.

"Oh, please don't worry," Melanie told her kindly. "For all you knew, we were never coming back."

"Here," said the woman, growing more and more at ease. She produced several other kitchen items from her person, tucked in various pockets of cloth, a couple wooden spoons, a spatula.

"Why don't you keep those?" Melanie suggested. "We've already brought new items down with us to replace them. We don't need them anymore."

The woman's face brightened slightly.

"Only if you are certain," she said.

"Definitely," said Melanie. "My guess is that you can use them more than we can right now."

CURTAINS

When she had left, I made tea and offered a mug to Melanie. We were standing in the living room where our tent was still set up under the open roof.

"It's amazing what people have done to survive," I commented, thinking through what the woman who had brought us back our curtains had likely endured to be able to stand on our doorstep that day. I did not know her particular story, of course, but I had heard enough stories from our Rwandese friends who had survived to know that nobody had an easy time of things during the genocide, no matter who they were or what their ethnic background was.

"It is, isn't it?" Melanie returned from behind me in the hallway somewhere. She stepped into the room and crossed in front of me, her arms filled with scraps of cloth and debris from one of the bedrooms to dump in the trash. I watched her, walking strong and determined. It was good to see.

The previous week she had been down with a bad flu virus of some sort and had been stuck in the tent for several days. It was awful seeing her so ill and not able to lie in a proper bed. Even so, she never complained. *What we have is so much better than the people at the camps,* she explained to me once, her voice weak with illness. I looked around at our house blown to bits with no windows, bullet holes in what was left of the ceiling, and water on the floor and could only shake my head in amazement at her grace in that situation. Just as soon as the fever had left her and she could be on her feet again, she had gotten right back in step with her former rhythm.

"You're amazing, you know that?" I told her, my heart swelling suddenly with inspiration.

She stopped mid-step to look at me. Her hair, usually so meticulously kept, was matted in places and she had smudges of dirt on her clothes. There was a spackle of something white on one of the lenses of her glasses. She swiped at her cheek with a shoulder like she was trying to wipe something off.

"What on earth are you talking about, Gary?"

"Well, you are. Just look at you, working so hard. And here you've just been so sick. Even so, you've still got the grace and the heart to give what you've got away to someone who needs it more." I paused to look gently at her. "Not too many women would put up with what you have, not voluntarily, anyway."

She sniffed a laugh. "Well. It's just what God has put in front of me," she said, pushing her way through the front door toward the trash.

When she was gone, I shook my head. "Even so," I said aloud.

We continued along, slowly making repairs to our house during the week and heading up to the camps over the weekends. Over time, the people who were left in Kigali began to meet back at the churches in order to find friends and pray to God together. Slowly, people began rebuilding their church communities. During the week we checked in frequently with our people in order to monitor the progress of the work everyone was doing to rebuild. It was here that I met Felicien.

Felicien is a kind man, gentle but resolved. By the look of his face and posture, I guess he is somewhere in his 30s. He is Hutu, standing at about 5'6". Even so, he narrowly avoided being killed himself by refusing to take up a machete against his neighbors. When the militia came in and rounded him and others up, he was left for dead for several days.

"I have lost my family," he told me with hands held open. We were standing outside the doors to the church. I had talked with many like him that day. My heart was heavy with the sorrows of my Rwandese sisters and brothers.

"I am sorry to hear of your loss," I told him genuinely.

"My wife and my two children, a daughter and a son, they are young."

I looked at him curiously as he spoke of them in the present tense.

"Are they alive?"

He smiled distantly and looked at his empty hands.

"Before, I thought perhaps yes, but now…with the cholera outbreaks, I don't know anymore. I fear they are not."

"So they did not die here?"

"I do not think so. On the night we were separated, the fighting was intense. Everywhere was gunfire. People were running and shouting in the streets. Many fled together. We tried so hard to stay together. People were pushing and we were separated in the chaos. For days after that, I looked for their bodies and did not find them. I have to believe they made it across the border."

CURTAINS

As he spoke with me, his eyes were fixed across the street somewhere. Suddenly, he broke his gaze to look me in the eyes.

"I have heard you are up there regularly."

"Yes," I nodded, "but there are many people in those camps." Nearly two million, I had heard.

"Please," he said, "I will give you their names. I do not expect you to find them, but if you do, please tell them I am here."

"Of course," I said, feeling that familiar feeling within the pit of my stomach. As the weeks flew by, many people had asked me to find their loved ones. And while Alexi and I had been able to match a few people up, the larger part of my list was still intact. As grim as it sounded, the stark reality was that it was likely they had been killed, if not in the fighting then by starvation or disease. I could see by his eyes that he knew this, too.

REUNION

NOVEMBER 1994
NEAR GOMA, CONGO (DRC)

"Whoa," came a young voice from the backseat as a large truck passed our car on the tar road. The truck had been going at top speed and nearly pushed us off the road with its recklessness. I remained quiet, choosing to keep my own commentary to myself.

"He must be in a hurry," Melanie said brightly to the owner of the voice, along with her four brothers and sisters. All five of them were crowded into the back seat, sharing seat belts and pressed together like sardines in a tin. I glanced at them in the rearview mirror and saw eyes wide with wonder and focused out the side windows.

When nobody responded to her comment, Melanie glanced sideways at me.

"I can't wait to see her face," she beamed. She practically sang with excitement.

I grinned. This is what it was all about. The small but significant victories. For weeks, we had been going between the camps, matching up the names of the missing. When we found the children—all from the same family and all still together and alive—we could hardly believe it ourselves.

"And your mother is Josephine Z?" we asked them. They nodded eagerly.

"Have you found her?" asked the oldest—a girl, no more than ten years old at best.

We were hesitant to commit. We wanted to make sure. Getting their hopes up only to have to backtrack later and tell them we had made a mistake would be cruel.

"We are not sure yet," we had told them the previous week, glancing back and forth, eyeing our list. "We need to check on some things. We'll be back."

We left them soon after and drove to the next camp. She was there in Goma, Alexi assured us. He had seen her with his own eyes only a few days before with some of the people from the church back in Kigali.

"Where is she now?" Melanie asked, eager to tell her the good news that her children had been found.

Alexi fanned his hand out across the sea of tents spread out across the volcanic plain, damp from the misty, gray air.

"Your guess is as good as mine."

We held a small service there later that day, in hopes that she would show up. When she did not, we asked around for her. One woman who said she was a friend said she would deliver the news to her.

"She will be so happy," she said with a gentle smile, almost as if she had no more energy to spare than that. "I will tell her," she assured us.

It was late in the day by then, so we left it in her friends' hands and headed back to the place where we were staying. The next morning, we headed back to Kigali, where we worked feverishly on our house and the local church for the duration of the week.

I did see Felicien once, and we nodded somberly at each other. He knew we would tell him if we had any news.

When the weekend came back around, we loaded up the Corolla once again and headed back over the border. We made straight for the children.

They were hesitant at first. One thing that the war had taught them was to not trust just anyone.

"We want to take you to find your mother," we told them in Kinyarwanda.

They blinked at us as if they did not fully understand what we were saying. The younger ones stood close to the older children, grabbing onto dirt-stained skirts and T-shirts for safety. The hair on their heads, usually cropped close to their scalps to prevent trouble with lice had begun to grow out, showing a dark crown of a couple inches or more on each of them. Their faces were thin, but not entirely malnourished. They had been eating, although perhaps not nearly enough. It was clear they had done their best to care for each other, an act revealed in the tenderness with which they handled one other. They were a family unit, even in their brokenness.

As she looked them over, an increasingly determined Melanie began ushering them toward the car, her face bright and relaxed. Her years of practice from having worked with children gave her a certain confidence and gentleness and soon the children began to warm to her. Once they were all buckled safely into the back seat, Melanie gently continued to talk with them, even going so far as to sing a couple of children's songs with them. Of course, these kids had been through much and it was difficult for them to sing, let alone smile. In truth, it was difficult for them to act like... children.

As we neared the Goma camp after a couple of hours in the car, Melanie reached out and squeezed my right hand, still on the wheel.

"Let's go make someone's day," she said.

We pulled up to the area where we knew we would find Alexi and I got out.

"Let's stay here for just a little while," Melanie said to the kids in the backseat. They blinked back at her, compliant and expectant.

It took a little looking, but I soon recognized a figure jogging up to me through a row of tents and plastic containers. Several men and women sitting nearby watched us with interest. The air was thick with the smell of cooking fires and crowded humanity.

"I saw the car," he said, somewhat out of breath. In his hands he held a clipboard with the names he had been collecting. "Are they here?"

I nodded once.

"OK," he clapped. "Bring them here. I will go find her and meet you back at this point."

Once I made it back to where I could make eye contact with Melanie, I waved a hand at her, indicating that they could come out. Her door flew open quickly and she was helping with the belts and soon she and the children were following along behind me at a hurried pace. When I made it back to the end of the row of tents where I had stood before, I looked around for Alexi.

"He said he'd be right back," I explained.

"He'll come," she said.

We waited for several more minutes standing like that. The children, to their credit, were immensely well behaved and waited patiently with us, hardly speaking to one another and certainly not causing any sort of disruption whatsoever. The oldest daughter had the two youngest by the hands, while the two middle boys stood quietly and pushed at the dirt with their toes.

When I saw him moving back down the row toward us, this time with a woman beside him, I felt something flip in my stomach. I can only describe it as joy.

As we watched, the woman walking with him stopped suddenly in her tracks, her eyes wide and fixed on the children. Her hand involuntarily clamped over her mouth as she processed what she was seeing. For one glorious moment, she stared at them as her eyes filled with water and her brow seemed like it would rise into her hairline for good. And then, as if nothing in this world could have stopped her momentum, she ran to them.

The children, though they expected to see her, stared at their mother as they, too, processed how she had changed since they had been separated. It had been nearly six months. Was this thin, gaunt woman dressed in rags their mother? And then, just as quick as the question was asked in their minds, recognition clicked and it was answered. Their faces glowed and their eyes brightened and they opened their arms to take her in.

"*Mama!*" They called, their voices filled with the joy of the moment.

The six of them held onto each other in a giant hug while the mother wept openly and spoke to each of them, cradling their faces in her hands and kissing their cheeks.

Melanie, Alexi and I stood back, grinning like idiots and watching through our own moist eyes too choked up to say anything of meaning, but not wanting to miss out on even a second of the reunion.

Yes, indeed. It was a sight to see.

FOUND

JANUARY 1995
NEAR GOMA, CONGO (DRC)

It took us six months to rebuild the house. As roofing is my specialty, I installed the roof first to keep the rain from damaging the rest of the work that needed to be done. Little by little, we restored the windows, the walls and the floors. All the while, we continued to make the circuit between the camps in Uganda and in Congo and then back home to Kigali. Our returns were marked by load after load of materials brought back from Kampala, the yellow Corolla practically groaning with the weight. While the stores in Rwanda would one day reopen for business, that day was still in the indeterminable future.

Throughout these months we continued to spend time at the refugee camps on the weekends, helping where we could. Some days it felt like an impossible mission, and still others made it worth it all. Alexi had been critical to this. Still based in Rwanguba, he was collecting names of people who had been separated from their families and organizing reunions across the bordersof the various countries.. We would then take letters between the camps and help people establish communications. In this way, we were able to reunite children with their parents, husbands with wives, sisters with brothers. These reunions were filled with joy, making the witnessing of such an event worth enough satisfaction for a lifetime for either Melanie or me. We loved doing it, and we were thankful that we could be in a position to help these people find each other.

Even so, aside from the occasional reunion of a mother to her children, Rwandans are consistently unemotional in public, and tend more often than not to stifle the public face of their excitement, even when they had not seen each other for some time. For example, once we reunited a couple who had been separated only a few months after their marriage. The husband was still in Kigali, whereas the wife was in a refugee camp. We drove her across the border and down into Kigali to the house where her husband had communicated to us that he was now living—all in all about a five-hour trip. Expecting at least some measure of visible excitement between the two newlyweds, we were somewhat floored to see the woman get out of the car, walk up the sidewalk to the house where the man was coming out to greet her...by handshake.

But it would be the discovery of Felicien's wife that would confound me the most.

Alexi was the one who found her.

"She's here," he informed me as Melanie and I unloaded the supplies we had brought to the camp from our stop in Kampala. The sun was shining brightly having only recently triumphed over the rainy season. I set a heavy bin on the dry, dark ground and looked up at his face. He was smiling.

"Who?"

"Claudina."

It took me a few moments to realize who he was talking about.

"Oh. *Oh!*"

He clapped my shoulder in his hand, his eyes bright.

"Come. I will take you to her."

Quickly, I explained to Melanie where I was going and gathered up some tools to take into the camp. On a whim, I grabbed my video camera and followed Alexi in through the rows of tents lined with people. After nearly a ten-minute hike in, we found her sitting in front of a smoking fire, stirring at a pot of porridge. She wore an orange T-shirt worn thin at the shoulders and a long wraparound skirt that matched the color of the dark earth. Her hair was pulled taut back into a scarf. She looked up at us as we approached. Recognizing Alexi, she nodded to him.

Kneeling close to the ground beside her, Alexi explained who I was and that I had been sent to find her on Felicien's behalf. Thinking she would be overjoyed, I began to explain to her that we could take her back with us that very weekend if she wished. Felicien was doing well and...

"You want me to go back...to Kigali?" She interrupted, looking at me, wide-eyed.

I nodded excitedly.

"Yes. We're leaving tomorrow," I answered. She could leave behind the crowded refugee camp, the stench of human waste, the disease, and the struggle for food. She was no longer lost. She had been found. *Found!*

She began shaking her head, clutching herself in her arms and rocking slowly.

"How can it be true?" she asked, speaking more to the fire than to either of us.

"It is true," Alexi assured her.

"We'll be back tomorrow afternoon. You'll be ready then?" I asked her, eagerly. I could hardly wait to see Felicien's face when we showed up with her.

"How can I?" She said, straightening suddenly. She looked back and forth between us, suspiciously. Alexi and I glanced at each other.

"It is OK," Alexi told her. "You are safe there now. It is over."

"No," she continued to mutter.

"The fighting is over," I said.

"No, it's just not possible," she told us. And then pausing she placed a hand over her chest, "Felicien?"

"I'm telling you," I told her, "I've seen him myself. He's back at the church. He has a place to live and he is waiting for you."

"No," she insisted. "Everybody knows you can't just go back into Rwanda. I will be killed the moment I cross the border."

"No, it's not like that anymore," I told her. I could hardly believe that she did not trust what we were telling her. Did she not want to leave the refugee camp? It didn't make sense.

"The ex-soldiers have been spreading lies here," Alexi explained. "You cannot believe what they tell you. We have been back and forth across the border many times. It is safe, I assure you."

She watched Alexi and me closely.

"No," she repeated. "I won't go."

We sat with her for several minutes more, trying to convince her that what we said was true, but in the end, she refused to go. Realizing that there was nothing more we could say to convince her, I popped the lens cap off my video camera and hit the power button.

"It's for Felicien," I told her, not without a hint of sadness. "He will be so happy to see that you are alive."

SEEING IS BELIEVING

JANUARY 1995
KIGALI, RWANDA

"I don't believe it," he said, his hands pressed to his mouth and still staring at the viewer on my camera where Claudina's dark face was frozen in front of a glistening tent tarp. "Praise be to God! I did not think it was possible."

"Oh, it's possible," I said with a smile, "And she is very much alive. Now if we could just convince her to come back with us."

Felicien leaned back in his chair, popping the wooden joints into a low groan. A series of clangs from the kitchen told me that Melanie had just finished with the clean-up from after our meal of beans and rice and was putting away the pots and pans. I had meant to help her when Felicien showed up at our gate unannounced. Somebody at the church had gotten our message to him and he had come as quickly as he could.

"Would you like more tea?" asked Melanie, rounding the corner into the dining room with a steaming teapot in hand. Felicien did not seem to hear her. She poured some into his cup anyway. We had offered him some of our dinner, but he said he had already eaten.

"It's incredible," he said. He turned to me then. "The, the children? They are well?"

Melanie and I glanced at each other. In all of the excitement, we had forgotten to ask about them.

"I'm sure...," Melanie began.

"We don't know," I finished for her. I remembered then, he had said he had a boy and a girl. They were young, two and four, as I recalled.

"We will find out," I quickly added, eager to make it right. His eyes flashed as he looked at me directly.

"You will go back there again, yes?"

"Yes, of course, this weekend. We will find her and tell her that you want her to come with us."

Melanie settled into her chair at the table.

"Perhaps if you will talk to her in the camera, maybe then she will be able to trust that you are safe and that what we are telling her is true," she suggested.

"But why will she not just believe you?" He asked, resting his hands palm upwards on the table. "She knows she can trust you."

"She has been told that people are being tricked into going back across the border," explained Melanie.

"Look, Felicien," I told him. "The soldiers there are feeding a lot of misinformation to the refugees. One of the things they are saying is that people are telling them it is safe to cross back into Rwanda, but that once they try to cross the border, they will be killed instantly. Just talk into the camera. Tell her that you're safe and that she should come back with us. She'll believe it if she sees you."

Felicien straightened in his chair.

"Yes, of course. I will do it," he said. "How?"

"Just talk to her," I said, grabbing the camera and clicking it back to life. "You are ready?"

"I am ready."

A WALK OF FAITH

AUGUST 1994-AUGUST 1995
KIGALI, RWANDA

Kigali had initially been a ghost town. The year moved along at a rapid pace as we reestablished communications and our lives in Kigali. So much pain had been absorbed into the Rwandan earth, that sometimes it felt as if the city itself were an open wound. Through that time, we held each other through the hard times and encouraged each other as best we could, always looking to God for strength when things around us seemed too heavy to carry.

We continued to spend the weeks back and forth at the camps, administering to needs where possible, as well as holding Sunday services.

People were looking desperately for God on the heels of what had happened to them. How could God have allowed such atrocities? Why was He letting His children suffer so? Where was He now? These were the questions people asked us. Each Sunday we drew large crowds as people sought to find the answers. Our message was always the same, we don't know why what happened did. All we knew was that God was still there. He was faithful to His children and that He could provide comfort even in the middle of the most horrible actions imaginable.

Once while I was at eating at a restaurant in Kigali, a woman approached me to ask if I had been at Don Bosco—saying that she recognized me. I told her I had and asked her how she had managed to survive. I knew that after the Belgian soldiers had left, the Interahamwe had rushed onto the grounds, killing many people immediately, but marching the vast majority of the 1500 or more Tutsis who had taken refuge there nearly two miles away to the hill at Nyanza. There, they were slaughtered en masse, mostly by being hacked to death.

"When the bodies fell, I fell with them," she said. "I pretended to be dead, too. I lay like that for a long time until I could get away."

I stared after her as she left our table, stunned that she had survived. In all, this made five people that I knew of who had survived that day. It was not long after our return that we received news from the Fergusons that three of the ten people I had helped smuggle to the Don Bosco School had managed to slip away from the group in the chaos and hid in the rafters of one of the buildings. While my heart rejoiced to hear the news, it was not, of course, without equal sorrow. Seven of the men had not been so lucky.

There was another at the school who I also knew had survived. It was the customs clerk who I had recognized and yet avoided, unable to face what I thought would become of him. I ran into him unexpectedly, on a downtown street, several months after our return.

"I saw you there," he said, after shaking my hand and smiling gently at me. "I am surprised to see that you came back."

Swelling with a surge of shame, I admitted that I had seen him there, too, and told him I was sorry that I had not said anything to him, or do anything for him.

"It was a crazy time," he said. "I do not blame you."

"I am sorry," I said.

"I am glad that you are back!" he replied.

I walked away feeling humbled at the thought that life so often does not turn out the way we expect and vowed never again turn away from somebody just because it feels uncomfortable.

Throughout this time, we continued to hear amazing stories of survival from the people with whom we spoke.

There was the Tutsi pastor, Enias, and his family who walked out of the country protected by his Hutu congregation members. They walked for days together, surrounding them like a human shield, faithfully protecting their friends until they had made it safely across the border.

There was one friend of mine who was forced to hide down the hole in an outhouse for days while bodies were thrown in and around him.

And then there was Anastaz, another pastor from our group. Anastaz is a remarkable man, standing only about three feet tall and with severely crippled legs and hands. Even so, he gets around well enough, despite an unmistakable hobble to his walk. But although he has many challenges physically, Anastaz is a gifted and much loved pastor. He is also Tutsi. When the killings began, the people in his church hid him behind a pile of about 1,000 mud blocks in a house next to the church. The blocks were separated from the interior wall of the house by about fourteen inches. Once he was inside, the church members piled benches and tables on top of the blocks and then walked away.

On the first day, sure enough, the mob came looking for him. They moved some of the blocks, but they couldn't find him. On the second day, they came back again and still could not find him. On the third day, they came back again. Finally on the sixth day Anastaz heard them say, "Look, this guy's crippled, we've got road blocks everywhere, there's no way he could have gotten out of here. He's got to be in here." And so, they dug through the blocks, and they found him.

They dragged him out, weak from hunger and stiff from being in such cramped quarters. The people had a club with nails that they were using for killing and were about ready to hit him over the head with it when Anastaz spoke up.

"What good is it going to do for you to kill me?" He asked. "I'm a cripple. I'm not going to go join the other army and fight against you."

And so he began to negotiate. He spoke with them for some time, and when it was all over, he had promised to pay them 2000 francs, the equivalent of USD $8.50, to let him live.

But while that mob was sent away, others would come.

Later, when another group came, he was taken to a hole where they were killing people and throwing them in. They told him to climb down into the hole, he said, "I'm not getting in there." So he sat on the edge, and again he negotiated. Incredibly, he was able to once again save his own life with another 2000 francs. After that, it was only a week later that the invading RPF army got to where he was and saved him.

Not all of the stories we heard were during the peak of the killing. Some were simply about surviving the refugee camps, such as in the story of one of the pastors from our group, Mugenzi Epaphriditus. He and his wife, Maria, had ended up in one of the refugee camps in Congo after many days of walking after their escape from Rwanda. At one point, World Relief had come in with $5,000 to help the refugee camps since the conditions were so dire. Acting as treasurer, Mugenzi was put in charge of that money. Before it was all used, however, the camp was forcibly broken up by soldiers and Mugenzi and Maria found themselves on the run, in charge $1000 cash remaining from the original $5000.

Knowing that it would be taken from them if it was carried loose in their clothing, they cleverly rolled the ten $100 bills into thin cords and braided them into Maria's hair. She put a scarf on top of her head and that was that. Later, when the soldiers searched the refugees for money, they never thought to look in her hair. Meanwhile, the two were on foot for weeks, boiling leaves to stay alive and refusing to spend the money for their own needs as it was not their own. When I ran into Mugenzi later after they had fled to Uganda before finally making it back down to Rwanda, it was the first thing he gave me, the remaining $1000.

I asked him why he had not used the money to buy food. "Because that is not what the money had been given to me for!" was his reply.

There were so many stories I had heard, and every time we encountered the people of the refugee camps we heard more and more incredible tales of survival, attesting to the inexplicable grace of God in the midst of such pain and suffering.

When Claudina finally agreed to ride with us across the border back down into Rwanda, we could hardly believe it. For six months she had been putting us off.

Over the months, we had taken extensive video of what life was like in Rwanda so that she would believe what we were telling her. When she told us that everybody knew there was no food in Rwanda, we taped Felicien and several others eating rice and steaming bowls of sauce with red beans and lumps of meat. When she said that she did not believe that it was safe to walk the streets of Kigali, we brought her back footage of members of her church community talking after church on Sunday and walking around in broad daylight. And when she said she knew she would be killed the moment she attempted to cross the border, we brought her back footage of other refugees crossing back into her home country.

During this time, she would watch the video in silence with sadness in her eyes, almost as if she could not allow herself even the slightest glimmer of hope. More than anything she wanted to go back, but she felt that it could not possibly be right. She had seen how it ended with her own eyes. The Rwanda she had been born and raised in would never return and to believe so was a pipe dream.

After our second visit, she had slipped us a note to return to Felicien. Felicien told us later that in the message, she described how the children had died in the cholera outbreak. He took the news with a stoic silence, but even he could not hide the grief in his eyes.

"She must come home," he said simply. "I will not stop trying."

When his months of sending messages back and forth through us finally paid off and she agreed to come back with us, Melanie and I felt a huge sense of relief. Claudina, on the other hand, felt quite the opposite.

As we parked the car on the border to be interviewed in one of two buildings meant for that purpose, I glanced at Claudina in the rearview mirror. Her eyes were huge and focused on the back of my seat. She wore the same orange T-shirt as when we had first found her in the refugee camp, as well as the same scarf on her head.

"You're going to be OK," I tried to encourage her. "They only want to ask you a few questions. We have to go in that building over there. You go to the one here. We can walk you to the door."

"This is it," she whispered from behind.

"No," sang Melanie, twisting in her seat to get a better look at her. "Claudina, I promise you that we would not bring you here if we thought that there was the slightest chance that there would be trouble. You are completely safe. Nobody is going to hurt you."

"I am going to die today." She took a sharp breath in, as if attempting to resolve herself to it. I got out of the car and opened Claudina's door.

"You are not going to die today," I told her gently.

She took my hand and got out of the seat, her face visibly a lighter shade than normal. She stood to her feet, her eyes racing from building to building. I closed the door behind her and retrieved her bag from the trunk of the car.

"They will want to inspect what you are carrying. That is all."

She took the handles into her hands, instantly foiling the handoff and dropping the bag onto the dirt. I picked it back up for her.

"Come on," Melanie told her, taking one arm. "We can walk you to the door."

We walked slowly and deliberately together toward the building. Halfway there, she dropped the bag again. Again, I picked it back up.

"You are going to be fine," I told her. "I promise."

We walked her to the doorway where she disappeared into the darkness within. As quickly as we could, Melanie and I trotted over to the building for foreigners, answered the series of questions we had by then memorized, and raced back over to meet Claudina just as she was emerging. She walked slowly, as before, but her countenance was visibly different. She stood straighter, taller. In her hand, she gripped her bag firmly. She was a new woman. She had been reborn.

Back in the car, she began to relax. Over the miles to Kigali, she began to ask more questions about the shape of things. Where was Felicien living? Did the church take much damage? We answered her questions, attempting to help pre-acclimate her to what she was about to return to. When we finally entered Kigali and drove to the house where her husband now lived, she got very quiet. I braked the car to a halt outside of a small mud and brick structure. Within seconds, the door flew open and Felicien emerged. She was fumbling with the handle and out her door before I could even unbuckle my seatbelt.

In all of our months of matching up broken families, we had seen a gamut of reactions. As I've pointed out before, the Rwandan people do not generally show emotion publicly. I am happy to report that the joy of Felicien and Claudina's reunion was too strong to be mitigated by cultural mores, because when they saw each other after almost a year apart, they did not walk to each other—they flew.

THE FUTURE

AUGUST 1995
KIGALI, RWANDA

"Gary?"

"I'm in here," I called. I was sitting in the office at my desk, mercifully still there after all of the looting of our house. Slowly, things were beginning to come back together. Both the phones and the electricity had by now been restored. Looking around the room now with a bulb burning into the night, I could almost believe that nothing had ever happened were it not for the smell of fresh paint and the bullet holes. But of course, that was not true. It had happened. Nothing was the same, nor would it ever be again.

"Can I talk to you for a minute?"

"Sure, Babes." I was rereading a letter we had received earlier that day from headquarters and I was working on formulating a response.

"No, I mean in here."

"Oh, OK."

I tossed the letter down onto the desk and padded my way down the hall toward the bedroom. She was sitting on the edge of the bed. She had a funny look on her face—kind of half smiling, half trying not to cry.

"What is it?" I asked, leaning on the doorframe.

"I have something to tell you," she began. One of her hands was holding the other.

"What?"

I was beginning to grow nervous.

She continued to look up at me, holding the words in until all of a sudden they spilled out.

"I think we're going to have a baby," she said, the corners of her mouth stretching up and out.

"We're...what?"

She nodded and I felt my stomach flutter.

"You're sure?"

"Well, not 100%, but almost. I want to see Connie when we're back up in Kampala."

I stood frozen in the doorway.

"Well?" She asked. "Are you excited?"

"Am I...?" I shook myself and crossed the floor in two steps toward her. When I reached her, I pulled her up off the bed, held her close to my chest and spun her around.

"Aack!" She yelled, laughing the whole time. "I don't think that's what you're supposed to do when you're pregnant!"

I continued to laugh and hold her tightly. I didn't care. I felt an amazing surge of emotion. All I knew was that everything was about to change for the better.

We stayed up late that night—well past missionary midnight—talking and planning our future. Our *future*, I kept thinking. I had been so moored by what was directly in front of us, and here we were talking about our future. It was exhilarating, intoxicating, even. I could hardly wait to tell our families. Everybody was going to be so excited.

The next morning, we woke up early, loaded up the Corolla and headed up to the hospital in Kampala where our good friend Connie worked as a nurse. One short visit to a small white office and Melanie's suspicions were confirmed. She was, indeed, pregnant. And if our calculations were correct, it appeared that our baby would be due in April, two full years after the start of the genocide. In that moment, I was filled with a feeling that I had not allowed myself to feel for several months: hope. And it was beautiful.

We spent the rest of the day pitching in where we could around the hospital. I would usually take care of maintenance issues when I came up, and that day was no different. Later that afternoon, we headed back to the apartment we stayed in while we were there.

"Are you tired?" I asked Melanie, worrying over her.

She laughed and leveled a look at me.

"Oh, no you don't," she said. "I am not going to be one of those women that flops down on the couch for the term of her pregnancy. Although..."

"What?"

"I wouldn't mind a pizza right about now. Ooh, no. Indian food. Something spicy. Maybe some mint chip ice cream?"

I laughed.

"Oh boy," I teased. "Here we go."

A BUSINESS VENTURE

SEPTEMBER 1995
KIGALI, RWANDA

It was early on a Saturday morning when we headed over to the Goma camp. We found Alexi already hard at work and talking to the people stuck there. It seemed his energy was limitless. He never grew tired of trying to collect names, discover needs, or talk with people.

When he saw us approach, he looked up at us and nodded. He was kneeling with a man, wearied from his journey and with holes in his thin brown pants. They had been praying together.

"Hello, Gary, Melanie," he said. He looked up at Melanie. "You are feeling well?" He asked.

She nodded and shot me a quick sideways smile.

"Agata sends greetings," he said.

"Tell her we are excited to see her, too. We may stop in this evening."

Alexi nodded slowly before indicating toward the man seated beside him.

"I have been talking with this man. He knows many people I know. He is a friend who loves the Lord. Praise be to God."

I smiled at the man and Alexi rose to his feet. When he reached us, he held out his hand.

"Are you ready?" he asked.

Melanie and I smiled. We had been coordinating our actions for the day for some time, going back and forth between headquarters and the small group of women we had been talking with at the camp.

"We have the money," I told him. "Let's do it."

We walked together over to where the small cluster of women lived. While many of the tents were poorly assembled, theirs were kept taught and neat, without the usual clutter of items surrounding the doorways or paths. One of the women—a young woman in her mid-twenties—sat outside tending a neat, strong fire under a pot. She stood when she saw us.

"Good news," Alexi informed her. "Your plan has been approved."

A shriek rose from a nearby tent and another woman, nearly twenty years older than the first, emerged from the doorway. A small child hung back behind her in the dark opening. The woman made straight for us and hugged Melanie tightly. "Praise God," she said. "We knew this day would come."

Melanie smiled broadly and waved at the child in the tent. Instantly, the little head popped back inside.

"Now, it is not a lot," I told her, "but it should be enough to get you started, perhaps to buy a bigger pot and some food."

"Yes, yes. Perfect," said the older woman. By now, another woman from across the narrow "street" had joined us. They chatted excitedly amongst themselves while I discretely handed over the small amount of cash we had been able to assemble.

The microloan—if one can call it that, for we never intended to get it back—wasn't much being only a hundred dollars or so. I had been asking what we could do to help for some time and they had finally told me that they could do a lot of good if they could offer a small food service to the people around them. They wanted to open a restaurant, they said. After some inquiry, they explained that while they could not cook anything elaborate, they could at the very least offer cooked porridge to their neighbors. They had no facilities, of course. No dishes; no chairs. People could come with their own bowls and pay a small amount for them to fill them. They would cook the porridge there outside their tents over the fire. Eventually, they could make enough that it would supplement their own food needs. They had children in their group, after all. They were growing and had needs of their own.

As we talked with the women further about the execution of their plan, I noticed after a while that Melanie was missing. Scanning the area around us, I finally spotted her sitting by the side of the older woman's tent. The little girl had finally ventured out and was now sitting in Melanie's lap and patting her hair. Melanie's arms were circled gently around the child and her eyes were closed. A slight smile played at her lips. She was happy there in that moment. At the same time, I knew she was also a million miles away.

HOPE COMES IN TINY BUNDLES

APRIL 1996
WINDOM, MN

In April of 1996—exactly two years after the beginning of one of the largest genocides the world has ever seen—our daughter, Melissa, was born to us. Returning to the States for the event, we were blessed to be surrounded by our families and friends. She was born on my mother Lillian's birthday which only added to the significance of her birth.

"I can't believe it," Melanie said, looking up at me after the doctors and nurses had left us alone with our little bundle in the hospital room. "I'm a mommy."

She had wanted to have children of her own for so long. I had watched her now for years as she held the young lives with which she came in contact. I could see that she craved to be a mother and to hold a little life of her own in her arms. But of course, even then I knew that our baby wasn't our own. She was a gift from God and ultimately she belonged to Him. I knew Melanie knew this, too, and felt blessed beyond words that she had been entrusted to take care of such a being. Seeing her like that made my own heart swell with joy and I reached out to stroke Melissa's cheek. In that moment, I knew beyond a shadow of a doubt that we had reason to hope. It was all I could do to keep from tearing up just from sheer thankfulness.

Melanie nursed her into a lively and happy toddler. When we went back, Melissa thrived in the Rwandan air, and was doted over by our church community there. Her presence—the presence of new life and hope—helped bring a smile to so many people who needed one.

Not to fly solo for long, she was soon followed by our second daughter, Megan, two and a half years behind her. Once again, we returned to the States where we could be near a reliable medical system for her birth. We did our normal schedule of visiting supporting churches and returned to Rwanda when Megan was four months old in order to introduce our newest family member to her home.

Together, they brought with them a sense of joy and healing I had thought unreachable before.

Slowly, over time, we watched the people around us on their pathway to healing, as well. So many of us witnessed horrific things and will never be able to fully reclaim the relative innocence of life before the genocide. Even so, we hold onto each other through the pain and daily vow to ourselves and to each other that we will not allow such things to happen again in our lifetimes. We have a responsibility. When Jesus came, He taught us to love our neighbors and, above all, to forgive. This is the message we teach. This is the message we *must* teach—not only for ourselves, but for the generations to come.

We had come through one of the most horrific events in history. We had lost countless friends and acquaintances in brutal and unfathomable ways. Our house had been destroyed. Our mission had been torn to shreds. Pastors and churches that existed to spread the good news of God's love had been scattered. We had been through an evil so palpable it hung thick in the air and stuck to everything it touched like an oily film. On the other side, with our growing family and remaining friends, we could not possibly feel more blessed. How could we know that there was yet another trial waiting for us around the corner? And where in our hearts could we fit any more sorrow?

AN UNEXPECTED TURN

DECEMBER 1999
ROCHESTER, MN

The Mayo Clinic in Rochester, Minnesota takes up a large part of the downtown area with its 15 million square feet of buildings interconnected by skyways and landscaped sidewalks. Its modern design is reminiscently Scandinavian with floors, walls and cabinets planked in natural wood and entire walls constructed from large chrome-framed windows. It is breathtakingly beautiful, populated by world-class physicians, run like a Swiss watch and is absolutely immaculate. And it was the last place in the world that I wanted to be.

"Are you feeling OK?" I asked Melanie, sitting beside me in the oncologist's office.

Melanie tilted her head and looked at me, deadpan.

"I'm fine," she said. "Stop worrying."

"Well?" I said, attempting to refocus my attention in front of us. My eyes grazed over family photos, folders, neatly stacked medical journals and framed diplomas. A healthy potted plant spilling vines of rounded leaves in suspension over the wood plank floor sat lushly on a stand behind the desk.

While we had still been in Rwanda, Melanie had finished nursing Megan when she discovered the lump in her one of her breasts. Thinking very little of it, she continued on with life as normal for several weeks before finally going to see a doctor at the Belgian embassy. Since there were no mammogram machines in the country at the time, the doctor took an inconclusive ultrasound and sent her on her way, unconcerned due to her lack of a family history with breast cancer. Later, though, she and I talked it through and decided to err on the side of safety. It was at that point, we decided that we should make a trip to Kampala where they had a better medical facility. Our friend and colleague, Connie, had moved there and volunteered to make all of the arrangements. Neither of us was particularly worried about it at the time, but when the results came back, we were advised to immediately return to the States. After a ten-hour trip back to Kigali and a day wrapping up loose ends, we boarded a plane and went home in the middle of winter.

Sitting in this doctor's office, I thought about the girls back in Windom staying with family while we sat in the clinic miles from where they were. I wondered what they were doing. Were they missing us? Melissa was three now and Megan had just celebrated her first birthday. It was December now and cold. We didn't even have any warm clothes for them. People from the church had been passing us little sweaters and coats.

"Stop worrying," she repeated.

I shook my head at the impossibility of the task she was asking and continued to stare at the plant. It seemed so healthy, *too* healthy. I wondered if that was the point. Had the physician chosen that plant herself to inspire patients with its healthful appearance? Or had an office manager chosen it? Did every office on that floor contain an identical healthy plant?

I tapped my heels on the wood floor a few times. She reached out a hand and settled it on my knee. I stopped tapping.

A soft knock behind us signaled the doctor's arrival and I straightened slightly. She greeted us gently and took a seat behind her desk, her medium frame easing back into the ergonomically correct black chair as if she were very much at home there. She was Indian by her facial features and accent, but had explained to us earlier that she had grown up in none other than Kampala, Uganda, where her family operated a business. This gave us a measure of comfort, somehow.

Her gentle eyes were fixed on Melanie.

"I'm afraid the mass is malignant," she said, referencing a photo she held in her hand from the test they had taken. "You are going to need treatment."

We stared at her, stunned by what she was saying.

"You're sure?" I asked.

She nodded and quickly moved on to our options, but I was still stuck on what that actually meant for Melanie.

AN UNEXPECTED TURN

Malignant.... The mass is... *malignant!* How was this possible? She was so young, so healthy. She took such great care of herself, how could this be?

I watched her in a blur as she began discussing things like "aggressive treatment" and the need for an "immediate surgical procedure." In my haze, I watched as Melanie asked questions, her mouth moving as if without sound. The two were talking, but I was not processing what they were saying. There were words, but it was as if I had been encompassed in a foreboding silence.

It was a silence and a numbness I recognized all too well.

After the meeting, we went home and tried to prepare ourselves for surgery. But of course, it wasn't normal. We were not in our home in Kigali. The girls were not used to the Minnesotan cold. There were restaurants and gleaming stores decorated for Christmas and people bundled in bright, fuzzy coats and hats walking outside in the snow.

And Melanie had breast cancer.

There was nothing normal about any of it.

The surgery was scheduled for Monday morning, December 13th. This gave us three days.

So, after a week back in the States, we left the girls once again with family back in Windom and drove back out to Mayo. The surgery went well. Unfortunately, while they were in there, they discovered that the cancer had spread to her lymph nodes. The surgery was not the end. Her battle had only just begun.

HALO

FEBRUARY 2000
WINDOM, MN

She lost her hair on a Sunday in February.

She was getting ready for church in the morning and it began to fall out in clumps. With the start of the New Year had come the start of the chemo treatments. For her, this meant sitting for three hours at a time while poison dripped into her body in hope it would kill any remaining cancer cells. And then three weeks later, she would go back to do it all again. This would go on for six months.

She did what she could, but the treatments left her nauseous and drained of all her energy. Even so, she never complained, pouring what little energy was left into her girls. She read them stories, played games with them and answered their endless questions. So it was with a fair amount of dismay when she began brushing her hair to discover a clump of hair was missing. And then another, and another. Every move she made to fix it only made it worse.

While she was trying to deal with her hair mess, she looked up to discover Melissa, our oldest, watching her from the doorway.

"You don't look like my mommy anymore," she said. "Where's my mommy?"

Unable to answer, Melanie, grief-stricken, stared at herself in the mirror. Just then, the phone rang. It was my new stepmother, Ruby. I explained to her what was going on.

"Now you just tell her not to worry about it," came Ruby's strong voice on the other end of the line. "Tell her to just throw a hat on her head and she'll be fine."

I thanked her and went into the other room where there was a bag of hats that a bunch of women in the church had donated for this moment. I took it to her. That morning when we arrived at church, we saw that a number of women—including Ruby—had come wearing hats.

None of it escaped her.

PULLING AWAY

JULY 2000
WINDOM, MN

Early on, Melanie had become dependent on the care of others. After only four days in the hospital, I had been taught how to strip the drain placed in her chest to keep fluids from building up and from that point on I was her lifeline. Along with the help of family, I took care of her and the children, as well as any other matters that needed attention. The girls did their best to show their support through this time, but her absence was taking its toll. It was hard. They began to pull away, gravitating toward my sister-in-law, who was so good about helping take care of them.

"Come here," Melanie called to Melissa as she skipped past our bedroom door one night. I had helped Melanie prop up a pile of pillows behind her in our bed, my bed, really. As we did not have a place of our own in Windom, we were staying in the room I had grown up in at my family's farm. But despite the familiarity I should have had with the place, it seemed unfamiliar somehow.

My dear mother had passed on only a couple of years before. We got the call from my brother Craig that she was desperately ill and we dropped everything in Rwanda to come back. We spent thirty hours on Christmas day flying across so many time zones only to arrive home shortly after she had passed away. Unable to face the pain of it, Dad pulled away from all of his kids, spending his days out with the trucks or just aimlessly driving around on country roads. Without her, the old farmhouse I had been raised in seemed empty. I searched for her presence but it was gone.

Melanie adjusted herself against the pillows as her energetic three-and-a-half year-old scrambled up onto the bed beside her. Melissa's long, dark curly hair fell haphazardly over her shoulders as she surged forward when a knee caught on the hem of her long, pink nightgown. Melanie winced almost imperceptibly as the bed lurched.

"Where's Megan?" Melanie asked.

"She's in the bathroom brushing her teeth." Melissa reared up straight and tall on her knees before suddenly allowing herself a free fall forward onto the mattress. Melanie grimaced from the jolt. The chemo was taking its toll on her energy and pain levels. Everything hurt.

"Melissa," I said, her name coming out more harshly than I had intended. "Please stop bouncing on the bed. You know it hurts Mommy."

In an effort to make up to her mommy, Melissa wiggled her warm body up next to Melanie's and gave her a kiss on the cheek. Melanie leaned her head sideways and nuzzled her oldest daughter.

"You smell so clean," she said.

"I just took a bath," she said proudly. "Aunt Melinda let us have bubbles, the strawberry kind." The kids were excited that Melanie's sister was there for a visit.

"And is Aunt Melinda helping Megan brush her teeth in the bathroom, or is she attempting this maneuver on her own?" She glanced up at me in the doorway with a spark of amusement.

"Yes," I laughed. "Megan is getting all sorts of help from Aunt Melinda. I believe they have not only brushed her teeth, but also the teeth of her dolly and last I heard, Big Bird."

Melanie nodded, clearly impressed.

"I was not aware Big Bird had teeth."

"Neither did I!" I added with a wise nod of the head. Melissa began giggling and started up bouncing excitedly on the bed once again, this time on all fours.

"Melissa," I reminded her.

Instantly, she dropped to a plank and rolled slowly off the bed, her feet preceding her with a thud.

"Why don't you go get a couple of stories for bedtime and bring them here," suggested Melanie gently.

"But I want Aunt Melinda to tuck us in tonight," Melissa pouted. "She's going to read *Little Bear*. The one about him being cold and needing a hat and coat."

Melanie hesitated. I knew she wanted to argue, to tell them to bring the books back and she would read them just like she used to. Instead, she nodded.

"OK. We'll do it tomorrow night. I love you."

"I love you too, Mommy!" yelled Melissa in a flurry of excitement. And just like that, she was gone. We listened to her little feet storm down the hallway, presumably to oversee her younger sister and the dental hygiene of one large bird. There was a pause and then a fit of giggles from the bathroom doorway. We listened as Melinda shuffled them on down the hall to the room they were staying in.

"I'll be there in a few minutes," I called after them. When things settled down a bit, I looked over at Melanie. She was pushing at a cuticle.

"They don't mean it," I told her gently. "It's going to be OK."

Melanie smiled at her hands.

"I know," she said. "And I'm so grateful for my sister—and for Diane, too," she said, referencing my brother's wife who also had so many times dropped what she was doing to come help out, despite the fact that she had three children of her own at home. "I can't even tell you how grateful I am. They are so dear to me. It's just, well, I miss doing all the things that a good mom does for her little girls. I miss being their mommy."

I pushed off the doorway and was at her side in an instant.

"You are still their mommy," I told her sternly. She looked up at me.

"I know. It's just hard not being able to do things for them. Like give them a bath or...brush Big Bird's teeth." She sniffed a laugh, as good-natured as it was helpless.

I put an arm around her behind her neck and touched her forehead with my own. We had been through the worst together more than once already and had come through the other side, together and still intact. This would not be any different.

"You'll get there again."

She nodded.

"I'll get there again."

NOT AFRAID

AUGUST 2000 – MAY 2001
WINDOM, MN

By the time August rolled back around, we went for six weeks of daily radiation treatment in Sioux Falls, South Dakota. It was about this time she developed severe neck pain. In October, I took her back to Mayo, but not finding a reason for the trouble in her neck, they sent her back home.

Over the following months, we continued to go back to Mayo—roughly once a month—while the doctors attempted to determine what was causing the severe pain in her neck.

"It's psychosomatic," one doctor told her. Melanie had been living with heavy pain in her neck for several months at this point. "You are having these fake neck pains because you don't want to go back to Rwanda."

We considered what he told us, but determined that it made no sense. When December came back around, we began making trips to Iowa to see a well-known chiropractor in search of some relief. Meanwhile, our mission put out a plea for three days of praying and fasting for Melanie. I can't emphasize it enough: people were so, so good to us.

From January to March 2001, we made three more trips to Mayo for more tests. In April, I left Melanie and the girls with Grandpa and Grammy Baker, Melanie's folks, and went back to Rwanda for three weeks to help out with some mission issues. When I came back, I was startled by how much she had deteriorated. On the trip back home, we swung back by the chiropractor in Iowa to see if he could help relieve her pain, but upon our arrival back in Windom, her pain had only increased.

Finally, on May 14th, we went to see our local family doctor in Windom, Dr. Mary Olson, for a refill on her pain medications. Dr. Olson had delivered both of our girls in the hospital in Windom and had been Melanie's doctor since the beginning.

"You need to go back over to Mayo," she told us after examining Melanie. By the way she said it, I knew something was very wrong, although Melanie didn't think anything of it. We went back. It was at that point they discovered that the cancer had metastasized into her bones. Her fourth vertebra was almost entirely destroyed.

Determining that any movement could cause the vertebra to rupture, they immediately brought in a stretcher, wheeled her away, and immobilized her neck.

"Once it comes back," her oncologist told us, "we don't talk about curing it anymore."

There were a lot of tears that night. I called her parents and told them. They were devastated, of course. In her hospital room after I talked to them, I held her as best I could past the contraption they had put her in to keep her from moving her head.

"If you hadn't given me such a lifetime of happiness in such a short time," I told her through my tears, "this wouldn't have happened."

She smiled at my effort to make a joke through the worst of it, but I could see that she was putting on a brave face for me. She had been dealing with the cancer for more than a year now. She was tired.

They screwed a halo into her skull next, a large somewhat cumbersome frame to keep her head immobilized. Miraculously, she was for the first time in a long while free from neck pain. Her spirits began to lift and we began to laugh again. Little by little, I could see the old Melanie surfacing as she was able to focus outside of her pain.

At this point, we began to demand a straight answer from her doctors. How long, we wanted to know. Melanie looked him straight in the eye when she asked it.

"I've been through a lot in my life," she told him. "I've seen things people shouldn't have to ever see. And what I've learned is that I'm not afraid of dying. I just want to know how long I have so I can make the best of what I've got left."

Doctors are always reluctant to give that kind of information out, but we were finally able to get an answer.

"Six months," Melanie sighed when he had left the room. She sat still and was permanently stiffened by her halo in the hospital bed. The black ring around her forehead was reflecting the low light from the room. It was a poor excuse for the halo I imagined should have been there. It struck me then that it would not be long before she got her permanent one.

"Six months," I repeated quietly.

"Well, OK then. If it's God's will."

I looked at her, surprised.

"Let's pray," I said, feeling still that God was going to see her through this. She was so young—it just did not seem right. I dropped the bar on the side of the bed, sat down beside her and held her hand softly. I had grown fearful of hurting her. "Please, God," I pleaded, "Please heal her. Melissa and Megan need her. *I* need her." When I was done, tears streamed from my eyes and I looked over at her. She was smiling tenderly at me.

"Gary," she said softly, "you're the one who has told me a million times that nothing happens to us without God's permission. He knows what's going on. He's still in charge, Gary."

I blinked at her, startled. I knew the truth of what she was saying, but wanting to argue, nonetheless.

"We have six months," she said, her voice gentle, "Let's make them count."

WITH AND WITHOUT

MAY - JUNE 2001
WINDOM, MN

A few days later, I left her at the hospital and drove back home to Windom and straight to a real estate agent's office. It took some searching but finally I found a house that was within our means. It was small, but there was a bedroom for us and one for the girls. On Memorial Day, I brought her home from Mayo and took her to take a look. She was elated.

"I can't believe you did this," she told me after we left. "You're sneaky."

I laughed.

"Well, I know how much you've always wanted to have your own home."

"We can paint the girls' rooms," she said with a smile.

"Yep."

"Whatever color they want," she added.

"Whatever color they want," I said.

"And we don't even have to ask anyone for permission."

"No, we don't."

We made an offer on the house that Monday afternoon. The owner, who lived in California, took the offer within an hour. We went in to sign the papers the next morning. We moved in on Saturday.

We wasted no time getting the house fixed up. Melanie chose wallpaper and fabric for the curtains. As it turned out, the color the girls wanted for their rooms was purple, so purple paint was purchased. They could not have been more excited.

A couple of weeks later we made a trek back to Mayo, this time to see if they could fuse Melanie's vertebrae together so that she could get out of that halo. While it had helped her get out of the pain she had been in before, it was bulky and difficult to maneuver in. Even getting in and out of the car had been quite the challenge. Throughout the ordeal, Melanie never complained, always more concerned about how my taking care of her was affecting me.

While we were away, the ladies of the church got to work once again. In our absence, they came into the house, hung the wallpaper, made and hung curtains and painted the girls' rooms in glorious purple. Another church nearby had heard what was happening as well and took up an offering for us. They bought us a dishwasher.

It was the middle of June now, and we were hopeful that the doctors at Mayo would be able to help give Melanie some of her quality of life back. If they could fuse the vertebrae and put in a metal rod, she would be able to get around so much better. She would be able to hold her girls again without feeling like there was a metal barrier between them. She would not feel as if she barely recognized herself when she looked in her mirror. While she did not complain, there was no question that it was taking its toll on her. If they could find a way to remove the halo, she would be able to reclaim much of her life.

It was not to be so.

What they found during that visit was that the cancer was still growing within the vertebrae and that it was taking hold throughout her skeleton. It had not gotten better; it had gotten worse.

They hit her with more radiation then, which meant more time away from her girls and her home. During this time, her pain increased at a more general level, causing her entire body to throb with it. I would hold her as much as I dared through these times, not wanting to amplify the pain she was feeling by the pressure of my touch.

While I prayed daily that God would choose to heal her, she and I both knew that God does not always choose to work that way. We had seen all too closely how good people were not always spared. I knew that she was not afraid of death. She—like me—viewed our physical bodies as temporary. Both of us knew that an end to the body does not mean an end to the soul. It was through this mystery that we knew that God would protect her, even though her body here on Earth might not survive. She would be held close to God and protected in His arms through death. It was what our mission was all about. Jesus had died on the cross so that we might live. It was just as we had sung back at Don Bosco when our future was so uncertain. He is our hiding place.

You are my hiding place...Whenever I am afraid I will trust in You.

Even so, an anxiety began to grow within me that I dared not name. What would happen when she died? How could I raise Melissa and Megan without her? They needed their mom. Would she die alone? Even worse, if I was there when she died, how would I cope with watching her die? And the girls...would they be there to watch her die, too? I wanted to be there for her when she went. I wanted to be strong for her, and yet—how to be strong? How would I pick my feet up the next day, and the next day after that?

She may not have been afraid to die, it occurred to me then, but I was afraid to live without her.

NO REGRETS

JUNE 2001
WINDOM, MN

Soon after we returned home from Mayo, we were scheduled to speak at one of our supporting churches. We had not been speaking for some time, of course, but this was one of those engagements that had been made months in advance and we had never bothered to cancel.

"Are you sure you are up to this?" I asked her, slowing the car to a stop in one of the parking spots outside of the church. As she was held rigid by her apparatus, she could not turn to look at me easily. Still, she tried, her torso moving slightly in my direction.

"Absolutely," she said.

"You don't have to, you know. Say the word and I'll drive you home."

"Gary, how many times am I going to have to tell you to stop worrying over me?" She laughed. "Now stop. This is something I want to do."

Realizing she was quite set, I pushed my way out of the car and crossed in front to help her out of her side. Having to wear a metal grid that holds a person in place is bad enough without having to ride in a car wearing that thing. Getting in and out was always a bit of a feat. She leaned this way and that while I helped support her enough so that she could step out of the car on her own. Finally, she was free and we walked together up toward the front entrance of the church.

It was early, of course. That was by design. We wanted to speak with the pastor a little and set up before anyone else arrived. When we were done, we took our place on the platform off center from the pulpit. After a while, people began to trickle in until the sanctuary filled to a couple hundred people or more.

We sang some hymns together. I had been there a few times before, as they were one of our supporting churches and knew several people in the congregation. Several of them caught my eye and gave me a welcoming nod or a wave. When the pastor introduced us to the congregation, I reached out and took Melanie's hand.

"You're doing OK?" I whispered.

She squeezed my hand back in the affirmative.

Approaching the pulpit, I began to talk to the congregation about Rwanda and some of the projects we were doing, showing a few slides while I talked. People were always interested to hear about the aftermath of the genocide and what we were doing to help rebuild, so I addressed some of that. This particular church had always been generous in its support of our mission over there, seeming to grasp the importance of what was happening and how God was moving in the midst of such difficult times. When I was done, Melanie rose to her feet. I was not sure she would even want to speak, so I had left it open, but now she was on her feet and walking to the microphone. I stepped aside.

"God has been so good to me," she told the many faces watching her. She went on to talk a little about how God had blessed her through her work in Rwanda, even throughout the darkest days. And now, she had cancer, she told them, addressing her odd appearance in front of them. Even so, she felt that God had been good to her. Though she was young, she felt she had received a lifetime of blessing. She felt it in her very soul. She had lived the life she had been given to the fullest by following the Lord.

"I have no regrets," she told them, pausing to think it over for a moment. "No, not a single one."

There was hardly a dry eye in the place when she sat down, least of all mine. She had so much courage in the face of what she was going through. It penetrated me to my core.

After the service, many came up to us to tell us how moved they were by Melanie's testimony. She was gracious to every one of them, but I could see that she was tired. I thanked everyone and took her home.

After that, she continued to go downhill. We were scheduled to go back to Mayo at the first of August, but as we were preparing to leave, we received a call from her oncologist telling us that there was no reason for her to come in.

"There is nothing we can do," he told me over the phone, "I'm sorry."

That night we sat Melissa and Megan down and told them that Mommy was going to die. It was one of the hardest things I have ever had to do. At 2½, Megan did not really understand what we were telling her, but Melissa got it.

"No," she said. "That's not fair."

"No, it's not," I agreed. I was holding her close to my chest as Megan had cuddled her way up to Melanie's free side. Melanie stroked her brown curls at the side of her face while tears streamed from her eyes. Megan did not like to see her mommy crying and pulled away to look at her curiously.

"Mommy?" She asked.

Melanie attempted a feeble smile.

"Does that mean you won't get to see me when I get married?" Melissa asked, her five-year-old brain calculating far ahead what the ramifications would be. "How can I get married if you aren't there, too?"

We all had a good cry after that and Melanie promised that she would be watching from above if she was allowed to do that.

"I will always be with the two of you in here," Melanie told her, patting their chests with her hand. "Never forget that."

FRIENDS

JULY 2001
WINDOM, MN

It was late July in Minnesota and the earth sucked in the hot sun with the unquenchable thirst that comes from millennia of long, icy winters and short summers. The air was warm and dry and filled with the sounds of birds and breeze.

Melanie was resting on the sofa under a thin blanket to keep the cool from the air conditioner from becoming a bother. Her eyes were closed, but she was not sleeping as was evidenced by the occasional question she would call out to me in the next room.

"Were you able to get some more mustard at the store?"

"I did," I told her, forgetting for a moment where I had put it, and then remembering again.

"Did they say when they were going to get here?" She asked a minute later.

"Could be any time," I told her. I was in the kitchen putting together some iced tea from some of the Rwandan tea we had brought back with us. I had only recently loaded up the dishwasher and set it to run. The whir from the motor filled the kitchen as I measured out the sugar into a pitcher. In the backyard, I could hear the girls giggling as they flew high on their swing set.

"They're here!" called Melanie just as I was reaching for a wooden spoon to stir up my creation. I grabbed one quickly and stuck it into the pitcher, leaving it for later. I jogged to the door just as the doorbell rang.

"Sorry, we're fine with brushes, Tupperware and vacuum parts," I said, yanking open the door.

"Gary!" cried Mimi, her arms open wide. Behind her, Phil was just closing the driver's side door of the large RV as their children ran up the lawn toward the house, clearly grateful to be released from the moving vehicle.

"Hey Uncle Gary," they called. I could hardly believe how big they were growing. I tussled heads and jostled shoulders.

"The girls are in the back," I told them. "Go on back there and say hello."

"Is it OK to park this thing here?" Phil called from the curb.

"It's fine," I told him and gave him a thumbs up.

He crossed through the yard and up to our doorway.

"Good to see you, friend," he said, extending his hand and pulling me in for a hug. "How are you doing?"

Behind me I could hear Mimi and Melanie laughing over something and I held the door open for my old friend.

"Would you look at this place?" Phil said, his eyes looking over the walls and doorways. "Looks like you got a good one," he said.

"Needs some work," I said, "but it'll do."

Phil smiled broadly, looking around the room until his eyes settled on Melanie.

"Well now, what's this contraption? Gary told me they put you in a halo, but he didn't tell me it looked like this. I was expecting more of a golden floaty thing above your head," he teased.

Melanie rolled her eyes and Mimi nudged him on the shoulder.

"Don't you listen to a word he says Melanie. He's just jealous that he doesn't have one of those. He's a lot farther off from being allowed to wear a halo than you are."

Melanie laughed her eyes bright with the teasing.

"Wow, it's good to see you guys," she said, looking the two of them over. Mimi had changed the cut of her hair slightly since we saw her last, and Phil had changed the style of his glasses, but other than that, they were the same Phil and Mimi I had known for so very long.

"It's been too long, hasn't it?" agreed Mimi.

"I only saw a blur of the kids as they passed through here, but I can't believe how tall they've gotten. And that Leah—she's growing up so beautiful…"

FRIENDS

"Which reminds me," Mimi interrupted, "I need to go peek at your girls. Megan was a baby last I saw her!"

I pointed her toward the back door and she went outside to say hello to the girls, who erupted with squeals of delight the moment they laid eyes on her. Although we had not seen the Bjorklunds frequently, the girls knew them well through phone calls and cards—not to mention the many, many stories we told them about their "Aunt Mimi" and "Uncle Phil."

As a matter of fact, they felt that way about all of the missionaries with whom we had lived in Rwanda. By the time Laurie and Gary Scheer showed up a little later, followed shortly after by Scott and Cindy Mueller, the kids were worked into a frenzy of happiness.

Somehow in the midst of the excitement, I managed to remember to serve up—and stir, in the appropriate order—the iced tea. Along the way, the barbecue was lit and hamburgers were set on the grill and the ladies put together some nice salads and we had ourselves a lovely dinner outside in the backyard.

"I can't believe how healthy your cheeks look," Laurie told Melanie as we sat down to eat at a long, fold-out table we erected for the occasion. Next to her, Cindy nodded in agreement and poured out more tea for everyone. Somehow, a tablecloth had been found and places set without me even having to ask for help. I don't even know where they found that tablecloth. It was as if after only an hour in my home, those three women knew my cabinets and drawers better than I did.

Melanie raised her eyebrows in surprise.

"Well, I don't know about that," she said.

"But you do," said Mimi, pausing with a metal spoon in mid-air, hovering over a fruit salad that had magically been whipped up somewhere between my cabinets having been inventoried and my drawers reorganized. I helped Melanie push her folding chair forward over the grass toward the table.

Melanie smiled weakly at her friends.

"You guys are very sweet," she said.

"Nothing sweet about it," said Mimi, "just the truth."

The kids swept in from the swing set and there was a flurry of activity as plates were filled and items were cut to spec and ketchup was appropriately applied.

"I am convinced they think that ketchup is a food group," muttered Mimi as her son left the table, trudging off to join the other kids on a nearby blanket on the ground.

For the next hour, we laughed and bantered just the same as we always had. We reminisced about the happy days of Rwanda, recalling the days in Gisenyi when we had lived near Tudy and E.J. Kile. They asked about the many people we had known in common, and we grew sad together when they named somebody whom we had not been able to find or who we knew had died. I told them about Alexi working in the camps and about what an incredible example of Christ he had been to me. I told them about our old friend Rosa, who used to work for the Kiles, and how she had been found living in a nearby city with her eight children, safe and sound after the war. There was so much to tell and we talked and laughed well into the evening when we all suddenly realized that it was getting late and children needed to get to bed.

I showed Laurie and Gary to the guest room and pointed out some clean towels while the Bjorklunds excused themselves to their own mobile living quarters. Scott and Cindy left to stay with some friends of ours from the church. And slowly, we all quieted down.

By the time I climbed into bed, the house was dark and quiet and I thought for sure Melanie was asleep. She had to have been exhausted after all of the excitement. I looked over at her in the dark where she slept in the hospital bed that had been brought in for her and was surprised to see her eyes open and staring at the ceiling. She had a smile on her face.

"I'm so glad they came," she said. "Nothing could have made me happier."

**

The next morning we awoke to the wonderful smell of frying bread.

"No..." I said, still lying with my face sideways on my pillow.

"Oh yes," said Melanie beside me, "I do believe so."

I began to laugh. Leave it to Mimi. I helped Melanie sit up and we made for the kitchen to see it with our own eyes. Sure enough, she was standing

FRIENDS

in front of the stove with a spatula in one hand and making her famous French puffs.

"Well, good morning!" she said brightly when we caught her at it.

"Are you sure you guys don't want to just park that thing here for a while?" I teased.

Melanie pulled her robe around her and leaned slightly against the doorframe, laughing out of sheer joy.

"Oh, how we've missed you," she said.

Just then, Laurie popped her head into the kitchen, fully dressed and ready to go.

"Looks like I made it just in time," she said sweetly, just as we heard a knock at the door. I jogged across the house to let in the Muellers.

"Wow. You guys don't waste any time, do you?"

Cindy smiled broadly.

"Time," she said, "is far too precious to waste."

Scott nodded solemnly before adding, "Plus we heard Mimi was cooking."

I laughed as I closed the door behind them. Before we knew it, the kitchen table was filled with eggs and sausage and sugared puffs of fried dough and the air was filled with the sounds of how it was supposed to be: good friends laughing and talking together as if there had not been a day that had separated us.

After breakfast, Laurie, Mimi and Cindy sat down with Melanie to see what they could do to help her out while Gary, Phil and Scott helped me with a few household projects. In many ways, it was like old times. And of course, in many other ways, it wasn't. It was later that night when we would gather together in the living room while the kids were playing in their rooms and speak openly about what was happening to Melanie.

"We sure hate to see you going through this," Laurie told her, sitting on a chair next to the couch where we had made Melanie comfortable in a resting position. They had spent most of the day chatting and reminiscing together. And now Melanie was tired. She laughed quietly and sighed.

"Well, I won't lie. It's not the most fun I've had in life. But I'm doing all right. I'm not afraid."

"You're a strong woman," interjected Gary Scheer, to which everyone responded in the affirmative.

"I'm not strong at all, you guys know that. Any strength I have is borrowed from Him."

"Bless your heart, Honey," said Mimi. "You're an inspiration, I'll tell you that."

Conversation grew quiet as Melanie humbly declined to answer for several seconds.

"Remember how at Don Bosco, when the gunfire broke out and little Zachary was running out in the middle of it and you just jumped out and tackled him to the ground," asked Melanie.

We all laughed and Phil reenacted what that whole scene looked like with Mimi looking something akin to a linebacker by the end of his demonstration. Mimi just shook her head. "I told you, it was just what God put in front of me."

"That's it," said Melanie. "This is just what God has put in front of me. The only reason for me to be afraid is if I think too hard about it and start to worry about all of the unfinished things I have and take my eyes off what's right there in front of my eyes. And it's Him—He's what's right in front of me. And He is giving me the strength I need as I need it. I have to just take one moment at a time and keep my eyes looking straight ahead at Him."

I watched her as she spoke, lying on her back and speaking with her eyes wide open and aimed at the ceiling. But of course she wasn't looking at the ceiling. Hers was a gaze focused far beyond what any of us in that moment could fully comprehend.

PRAYER AND SINGING

AUGUST 2001
WINDOM, MN

By the middle of August, Melanie was in constant pain and required the use of morphine to help her cope. Throughout this and the previous months, people had been so good to us, volunteering their time to come help out with Melanie and with the girls. We had a guest room in our basement, which was rarely empty.

And then, I got an unexpected phone call. It was Laurie Scheer, now living in Denver with Gary and her family.

"I need to come out," she told me. "Is that all right with you?"

Knowing that it would cheer Melanie to see her old friend, I readily agreed. On August 18th, Saturday morning, she showed up. There wasn't anyone staying in the guestroom at that time, so it was a blessing to have her there. That night, she helped me move Melanie to the bed from the couch—not an easy task on my own. Melanie seemed cheered to see her there, but was relatively incoherent. Throughout the night, she mumbled words and phrases I could not understand.

In the morning, she perked up some and Laurie and I moved her back to the couch. Laurie said she would stay with her so that I could take the girls to church that morning, so I ambled off to help get them dressed and ready to go. Meanwhile, I got a call from my cousin Kim, who had worked as a hospice nurse. She wanted to help out with Melanie while we were at church, too. *Would that be all right?* Not long after I hung up with her, I got another call from Virgie Ostenson, a dear saint from our church. She, too, wanted to come help out and sit with Melanie for a while.

With those three saints graciously at Melanie's side, I gratefully took my girls away to church that morning. They had needed that—to get out and be amongst their friends and to feel a semblance of normality.

But of course, there was nothing normal about that day. At precisely 11:30 a.m. when the church service let out, Megan bumped her head hard against one of the pews. She let out a cry. As I was holding her, trying to console her, the pastor dismissed the service.

Soon after that, a couple miles away, one of the women from my house got into her vehicle and drove as quickly as she could toward the church. Bursting in through the front doors, she found the pastor greeting people as they exited the sanctuary and told him that she urgently needed to find me. My phone had been turned off and she could not get hold of me.

While the pastor called the people who were still there back into the sanctuary, Megan and Melissa were gently herded off by some of my friends. My pastor found me, and told me to sit down.

"Something has happened," he told me.

I remember little about the next several minutes, but it seemed to me the room seemed suddenly too small and too confined. I made it to my car soon after and drove home as fast as I dared.

I found her on the couch where I had left her, still surrounded by people who loved her. She looked so peaceful there. I could hardly believe at first that she was not just sleeping. It was not until I took her hand and spoke her name that I realized that she was actually gone....

While I wept, they told me of her peaceful last moments. They told me about how they had been singing with her and praying with her. At the end, my cousin who had been a hospice nurse looked up at her.

"I think she's gone," she had said. She got up to check her pulse to confirm it. It was exactly 11:30. She was thirty-four years old.

Over the next hours, people from the church came to say their goodbyes while arrangements were made. Throughout this time the house was filled with prayer and with singing. When the funeral director finally made his way there, he remarked on it.

"I have never been in a place where so many people were singing when someone had just died like that. It is clear that she was well-loved."

And she was. She truly was!

※ ※ ※

I have not told this story out of sadness. I have also not told this story to make death seem easy. It is not.

When I was younger, I remember believing that God would protect me from bodily harm if I asked earnestly enough for it. And while I do feel that there have been many times in my life when I felt His hand of protection, I am under no illusion that I am walking around in a safety bubble, protected from anything and everything life may throw at me. Mine is not a life of immunity from pain or trial.

What I do want to say is that I feel blessed. Having chosen a life as a missionary is not without risks. This goes without saying. I remember all too well the people who warned me about certain dangers that I would—and did—encounter on the field. In the end, though, death awaits each of us in our time. What happened with Melanie is a stark reminder of this. She could have chosen to live her life sitting at home where it was comfortable. Perhaps she would have been a schoolteacher in Pekin, Illinois where she grew up. Perhaps she would have made a large contribution at home in the church, inspiring people with her passion for the Lord and gentle spirit. There would have been nothing wrong with this. Even so, I can't help but think and be inspired by how she chose to do what was really in her heart—to go into a situation that was not "safe" and to be a light in the world. And in so doing, she brought joy and inspiration to so many people.

She could have left at any time. When the invasion happened in 1990, she could have easily said, "Well, that's enough for me." She did not have the years of history with the place that I did. It would have been easy for her to go home. She could have; and yet, she did not. She did not because she did not fear death. That would happen regardless of whether she stuck her neck out on the line. It was, as she put it, "in God's hands."

There is no question: Melanie lived her faith, each day, each hour.

And in the end, she had no regrets.

AFTERWORD

Much has been taken from me and much has been given.

While I am now able to look at what happened to Melanie with grace, it was not always necessarily so. For quite some time, I was in a tailspin. I grieved. I was angry. There were days I hardly felt as if I could cope. And yet, God was there for me, even in the midst of my darkest days.

When the girls and I considered going back to Rwanda, we knew things would be different. For one thing, we had a huge support group in Minnesota. People from the church went out of their way to help out. They watched the girls for me, they brought us food, and they held us up with their prayers. And yet, Rwanda continued to call. And, as I always seem to do, I went back.

Time passed. The girls grew. The girls missed their mom. They began to pray. They began to pray with fervor.

"Please God," they prayed, "Bring us a mother."

And yet, the years passed with no mother.

"Doesn't God hear our prayers?" Megan asked me when she was six and old enough to begin to put it all together. She was getting tall now, and her hair was full and curly just like Melanie's had been.

I wanted to know the answer to that myself. Years had gone by and I knew that I was ready to love again.

This was not discovered overnight. There were many tears and many dark nights that seemed like they had no end. But I knew, nonetheless, that

FAITH THROUGH FIRE: RWANDA AND ME

I was ready. I wanted somebody special in my life—almost as much as the girls did. God had answered my prayer before. Where was He now?

Meanwhile, across the waters in Japan, a woman was shopping in the produce section of a Japanese supermarket. She was wondering the exact same thing.

* * *

"Have I not given you my life in service?" She asks, angrily bagging up a head of red lettuce. "Have I not given you everything? And here I am, forty-three years-old, and too old to have children of my own."

As this conversation is going on in her head, she bags up the unfortunate lettuce somewhat violently and drops it in her cart, staring a hole into the produce section. They are large carrots, as she is used to seeing. Since she had become a missionary in Japan, she has gotten used to a lot of things, including being single. All the while, she believed that God would bring her someone to love and share her journey with in His time. And now, it is all folding in on her. *Her* time is ticking and there is no going back. She has delivered her part of the bargain. Where was His?

"If You loved me, You would give me a husband. All of my girlfriends have one by now. But you haven't and you obviously don't."

She has grown accustomed to the Lord answering her prayers—sometimes yes, sometimes no—but this was different. Was it a yes? Was it a solid no? She could accept a maybe, but she had wanted children...and that could only be delayed for so long.

Throughout her life, she has asked God to show her direction. Throughout her life, He has done so. And, as sometimes happens when people are accustomed to getting things they pray for, God has to remind us that He is in control, things happen according to His timing; not ours.

It is Christmastime and the Japanese supermarket is decorated accordingly. Over the loudspeakers, holiday music is playing on a loop throughout the store.

"I don't know any other way, but it's awfully hard to serve someone who doesn't love you," she mutters out loud.

Barbara knows she is being pouty, but she can't seem to help it. She loves her life as a missionary, but it is hard to be alone. She wants somebody to share her life with.

AFTERWORD

Just then, in the midst of the Christmas music, comes another kind of song. A musician herself, she recognizes it right away. It is a hymn.

It's no secret what God can do, come the familiar words. *What He's done for others, He'll do for you.*

Barbara stops, a sack of carrots in one hand and her other hand poised darkly over a radish.

With arms wide open, He'll welcome you. It's no secret what God can do.

It is not a Christmas hymn. It decidedly does not belong. In fact, it is a hymn she knows from home. But of course, she is not at home. She is in Japan, *in a supermarket!*

Tears begin to well in her eyes and she makes a beeline for the register. She begins to bawl. The clerk eyes her nervously, not sure what to do with this public display of emotion. The Japanese, like the Rwandese, are similar in this way.

"Are you OK?" he asks her.

She nods. Sniffs.

"This song is beautiful and it's speaking to my heart," she returns smoothly in Japanese. She has studied her language lessons well and can speak quite fluently after her years in the country.

"OK," he responds, and tells her how much she owes. "Now please leave the store."

She does and heads straight for her car.

In the car, she buries her head in her hands as the words from the hymn play over and over in her mind.

"Please forgive me, Lord. My experience tells me that You are not big enough, but my faith says You are."

"I know where you live and I know where you shop," the Lord says back to her.

"OK," she says. "I acknowledge that You are watching me. Please, then—send me a husband. I am so tired of being alone. Or, if not a husband, at least please bring me a dog."

Soon after, the Lord brings Barbara a cat.

* * *

It went on like this for some time, until one day nearly a year later, the Lord facilitated a meeting between us. It was on a Christian singles website. Like I said, I don't claim to understand the mystery of God's ways.

Over time, we got to know each other. We would leave video chat open and talk to each other throughout the day. She would join my girls and me in our daily devotions. I would talk with her about life throughout the day. We laughed together, talked together and prayed together.

We were a match in every way.

Today, Barbara is my rock. For her, the move to Kigali from Japan was an easy decision once we had decided to marry. The girls, although at first hesitant about having a stepmother due largely to tales of Cinderella and the like—in spite of their prayers to the contrary—came around quickly once they met her.

"Can we call you 'Mom' yet?" Melissa asked famously, once I had popped the question to her. There were many hugs and tears. The girls had fallen in love with her, as I had.

I thank God every day for bringing me Barb. She has brought healing to me and to my daughters—as well as joy to everyone who comes in contact with her bright personality. Gifted in music, she brings much to the ministry here in Rwanda. On the street and at the markets, she is known as "the lady who sings."

Recently, at a trip to the market, she was bartering with an elderly woman who was attempting to give her a price reserved for foreigners. Calmly, Barb looks at her and says, "I want to sing for you."

She sang one song, then another. By this time, quite a crowd had gathered around. Having studied opera at school, Barb is quite comfortable singing in front of a group of people, though, and sang clear and pure the words of God's love. Each song, the woman came down a notch in price. After three songs, the woman looks at her with a smile...and gave her the original price Barb had asked for.

Had she asked for one, the woman may have even thrown in a cat!

Gary distributing Gospel portions while visiting a rural church

Rosa

The Barge at Cyimbili

The Beard, 1976

Melanie with Melissa & Megan, Easter 2000

The Bennetts, April 2006

WorldVenture Team (early 1980s)
Left to right: Scheers, Kendells, Kyles, Websters, front: kids, Gary Bennett, Dick Jacobs

At Grammy's house in Pekin

Night view of Gary's front gate with view of Kigali

Melanie (Baker) Bennett
(1967-2001)

Made in the USA
Middletown, DE
28 July 2022